Multiple Campus

Scenarios for the University of the Future

Paolo Fusi

Introduction   The University and the Future of the City   5
Paolo Fusi

The Future   Multiple Campus   12
The Universität Hamburg of the Future   36
The Urban Campus: Von-Melle-Park & Bundesstraße   37
Klein Flottbek Campus   76
Science City Bahrenfeld   96
The University Medical Center Hamburg-Eppendorf   102

Appendix   Image Credits   110
Authors and Editors   111
Publication Information   112

The University and the Future of the City

Paolo Fusi

History and Future

In our culture and society, scholarship is the greatest asset that we possess. Preserving and maintaining this asset is a responsibility that we cannot neglect. In the future, however, scholarship will not only be the greatest strength of Western civilization, but it will also represent tangible opportunities in international competition. Reflecting on the future of scholarship and its design represents one of the greatest challenges of the present.

In the year 2019, the Universität Hamburg celebrated its one-hundredth anniversary. The centennial was not just an opportunity to look back at the past and celebrate its own history, but also provided an impetus for planning its future. For our reflections in the fields of architecture and urban planning, this event provided an excellent opportunity to delve into the topic of the development of university campus locations in connection to the future of the city.

The theoretical considerations and the design concepts introduced here are not meant to be seen as a completed project. Instead, they suggest idealized applications of a methodology. They should provide reference points for a planning discussion involving everyone who has a stake in the future of the campus locations.

The forward-thinking aspirations of the Universität Hamburg (united under the motto: "Where is scholarship headed?") and the thought that they are putting into planning the campus locations of the future provide great value to the entire city of Hamburg. Cities have always been an example of the most complex and fascinating expressions of civilization. Furthermore, cities intrinsically thrive from their strong cultural institutions. The city of the future, however, will need vibrant, capable, and excellent universities more than ever before in order to adequately fulfill their role in the development of humankind. For several years, we have been observing the ways in which university cities compete to distinguish themselves so they can win over new residents. Searching to develop themselves culturally and professionally, young people move to the cities where there are the most appealing opportunities for development. Yet there are others who are searching for the diverse cultural spectrum that is best developed through the synergetic effects of university cities and want to live in these places. However, cities grow and flourish not only based on the quantity of opportunities, but also the quality of life they can provide.

Cities provide better work opportunities and prospects for self-actualization: dynamic and creative entrepreneurs have better chances of finding the right employees here. Correspondingly, well-educated and capable workers receive better job offers here. At the same time, more attractive living conditions arise in these places due to the wide variety of cultural events and opportunities for personal development, leisure activities, and socializing. Even though the media and virtual forms of communication are continuously being expanded, meeting other people in person in the real world remains essential, or perhaps has even gained significance: as a way of compensating for the ephemeral dimension of social media.

Gathering together, meeting, interacting, working, and communicating at real locations are not things that happen automatically, nor can they take place just anywhere. The surrounding environment must be suitable and appealing, so people feel comfortable there and feel like they can fulfill themselves in these spaces. Of course, it is the

1
2
3

4
5

Introduction

1
View of the Universität Hamburg main building on Edmund-Siemers-Allee, ca. 1980

2
Lecture hall in the main building of the Universität Hamburg

3
Foyer on the east side of the main building of the Universität Hamburg

4
Urban Campus: Von-Melle-Park and Bundesstraße – Axonometric view of the Layers Scenario (see pp. 178-179)

5
Universität Hamburg, Von-Melle-Park Campus with the "Philosophers Tower" in the background and the auditorium to the right, early 1960s

responsibility of architects and urban planners to design a diverse range of suitable physical spaces.

For our reflections on this subject, the question of the physical, spatial, and morphological quality of the university sites in the city, especially in Hamburg, plays a central role, as well as the question of high-quality, urban spaces of the future. We have been dealing with the topic of the urban university campus for a long time, based on the conviction that the locations of the institutes in the city of the future will continue to play an even more important role in creating urban quality. At the same time, research concerning the university campus is part of a more comprehensive reflection on qualifying the morphological dimension of the city of the present and the future, as well as on the tools of architecture and urban design that enable us to shape it.

Goal and Concept: Our Thesis
Our research on the historical and current locations of the Universität Hamburg, as well as our investigations into future campus locations and their correlations with the city of Hamburg and the world, is conducted with the goal of drafting a concept for the development of their spatial and architectonic resources in the future. In doing so, intensive cooperation with the leadership of the Universität Hamburg is of fundamental importance.

The future concept for the university campus in Hamburg is based on developing the locations that have grown historically, along with their identities and their permanent structures within the urban space of Hamburg. We are convinced that a successful concept can only be developed in harmony with the historical identity of the city and the university and by integrating their shared strengths.

At the same time, the locations on the whole (Von-Melle-Park, Bundesstraße, Bahrenfeld, Klein Flottbek, and the University Medical Center Hamburg-Eppendorf) must be generally reformulated as a "Multiple Campus," which will indicate a significantly altered design. The "Multiple Campus" is a new form of university campus that we propose as a thesis but can also implement tangibly with action plans. Our work reflects on and defines the architectural and urban design tools that will shape the "Multiple Campus." Some of these tools are already available and are being implemented in project planning. Moreover, they have already been demonstrated by existing tendencies and we have represented them in the form of spatial concept diagrams.

The "Multiple Campus" concept is based on the conviction that strategic measures will bring about a major turning point in the history of campus architecture and urban design. With this transformation, the campus will be able to provide innovative and excellent infrastructure for the current and future requirements of research, education, and the transfer of knowledge. It will enable the scholars of the Universität Hamburg to become even more innovative and competitive on an international stage. At the same time, the university will become even more strongly integrated into the urban context of the city of Hamburg.

Strategic Tools
The implementation of this concept is enabled by the utilization of strategic and planning tools that are of equal importance for both the university and the city of Hamburg.

Primarily, this involves developing spatial and morphological designs for new, capable, and architecturally attractive urban spaces. These spaces, as well as their architectural and typological components, must be consistently positioned within their respective local context. Furthermore, they should make an innovative contribution toward future development.

It is equally important that the interpretation of these new spaces will be a historic opportunity to absorb the tension of their history, the defining identity, and the existing qualities of the campus, and project them into a new vision of the future.

To carry out this vision of the future, it will be strategically important to implement it in stages, to differentiate the spaces hierarchically, design flexibly, and to structure the mobility, services, and information dynamically.

It will be critically important to develop a planning process based on intense interdisciplinary cooperation in order to connect the planning competencies that are necessary with the strategic, political, and economic interests of everyone involved.

Permanent Structures, Heterotopias, and the "Multiple Campus"
In this concept, the term "Multiple Campus" is in essence a location where various types of space are produced and can develop synchronously.

We are undertaking a methodical effort to integrate several structuralist thoughts with post-structuralist perspectives. On the one hand, it is impossible for us to neglect the primary role of historically permanent elements. They represent essential morphological components that are necessary in order to generate continuity and a connection to the historical city, its identity, and its genius loci.

On the other hand, we are convinced that we can only reinterpret and reactivate these elements when additional aspects are also considered, dimensions such as multiplicity, complexity, and contradiction.

In our concept, the "Multiple Campus" is defined by clear, solid, permanent structures that guarantee to shape these spaces within the urban context on the long term, yet also allow for flexible repurposing. Moreover, these structures will be able to provide versatile spaces that will be at the disposal of multiple users and open to multiple perceptions simultaneously.

However, in our interpretation, the campus is very closely associated with the term "heterotopia" (as the concept is used by Michel Foucault in his

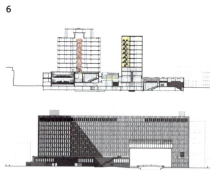

6

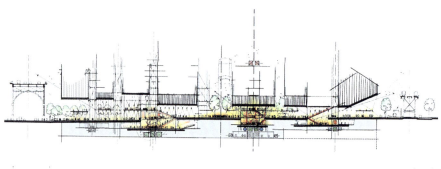

7

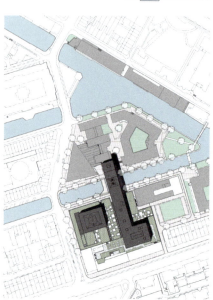

Introduction

6
University of Amsterdam Roeterseiland Campus: West-east cut, view from the east and site plan

7
Columbia University Manhattanville Campus in New York City: Cross-sectional view with the publicly accessible ground level marked, site plan of the completed southern part of the campus and a view of the first three buildings: Lenfest Center for the Arts, Jerome L. Greene Science Center, and The Forum

philosophical discourse). From this perspective, "heterotopias" are capable of uniting different spaces that are actually incompatible and placing them in relation to one another.

The "Multiple Campus" represents an innovative answer to the tendencies of our culture and our society. These are primarily shaped by the virtualization, digitization, and continuous developments in communication media, forms of knowledge and knowledge transfer, and they enable various phenomena to unfold at the same location simultaneously.

The "Multiple Campus" is conceived of as a location that will be capable of keeping up with the increasing complexity of our culture, adapting to the further differentiation between lifestyles in our society, and productively interpreting the dissolution of the boundaries between working (learning and researching), living, and leisure. These phenomena are being observed with increasing frequency, particularly in the lifestyles and working arrangements in creative or innovative fields (e.g., the IT sector or start-ups). However, they are also related to the innovative forms of education and research found at a University of Excellence. Furthermore, they share comparable processes and means of creatively developing and transferring knowledge. In the "Multiple Campus," it is possible that several activities with various participants could take place in the same space or in separate spaces, depending on what is needed.

Furthermore, the "Multiple Campus" provides the ideal context for "agile" management of spatial resources. This term, which describes an innovative form of business management, is here deliberately appropriated metaphorically, and we use it as a synonym for the continual reorganization of teams and rooms in the "Multiple Campus."

For us, "Multiple Campus" is a fundamentally versatile and open term, which takes its shape both in virtual and in physical space. The "Multiple Campus" of the Universität Hamburg will be implemented at different scales (macro, meso, and micro) in the city. At each of these levels, the "Multiple Campus" will take on the unique urban qualities of the various districts of Hamburg and can be implemented with specific identities for each individual location.

The Future

Multiple Campus   12
The Universität Hamburg of the Future   36
The Urban Campus: Von-Melle-Park & Bundesstraße   37
Klein Flottbek Campus   76
Science City Bahrenfeld   96
The University Medical Center Hamburg-Eppendorf   102

Multiple Campus

Scenarios for the Campus Sites of the Future

1

1
Universität Hamburg Urban Campus, Von-Melle-Park and Bundesstraße: 3D model, Layers Scenario (see p. 177)

The Term "Campus" in Architecture and Urban Design

The term "campus" is being used ever more frequently in architecture and urban design to describe a wide variety of places and contexts. Due to its usage in the debates within the discipline, the term "campus" is becoming more interesting, more complex, and richer in meaning. The fact that it is used in such varying contexts and situations demonstrates both the complex dimensions and diverse implications this term can adopt. Primarily, we are interested in the term as a type of space and as a tool for design in the discipline of architecture and urban planning. Reflecting on the campus should help us understand which architectural, spatial, and urban qualities can be made possible by this type of space, and how we can utilize it for our work in design. At the same time, the goal of this research and the application of the term "campus" specifically in connection with the Universität Hamburg (UHH) also includes elucidating how the campus infrastructure can help enhance the productive potential of research and instruction at the university. Additionally, one further goal is to find out how the urban campus in Hamburg can fulfill an even more important role in enriching and improving urban quality.

Our interest in this term is not new, and it comprises a wide range of aspects. In recent years, our research has already dealt with the close relationship between cultural locations and urban planning, as well as between buildings with cultural functions and architectural designs. Our investigation of the term "monument" and our intensive work with cultural structures, which play a monumental role in the urban context, are what led us to examine the subject of the university campus as well.

In order to address the overarching question of the present and future of the urban campus, it was necessary to first reflect on the history of the university, the Von-Melle-Park campus in the city of Hamburg, and the campus as a type of space.

We are convinced that the university bears enormous potential for the improvement of the urban quality of Hamburg. In order to truly make full use of this potential, however, one has to free oneself from the rhetoric of the city of Hamburg being opposed to culture and universities. Among all the experts in the field, it has long been clear that universities are an excellent driver of urban development. As a result, it is no longer the question of "whether" or "why" we deal with campus sites in the city, but "how" we deal with them.

As part of an ongoing examination of the current architectural and urban design debates in Hamburg (primarily densification, housing, and public space), we seized the tangible opportunity in recent years to work on the most important urban campus in Hamburg (Von-Melle-Park) and to take it as our laboratory for our reflections.[1] In the first step, we are going to adopt some of the essential results of the research on Von-Melle-Park and take them as a foundation for our further thoughts.

The current research on the "Multiple Campus" constitutes one further step in the context of a greater research project that is based on the assumption that design is an act of research in which our tools continue to be further refined and developed.

For our work as architects and urban planners, this work represents an opportunity to deal with the future of the city and to develop some reflections on its importance for our discipline. We are methodically attempting to integrate structuralist thoughts with poststructuralist perspectives. On the one hand, it is impossible for us to neglect the primary role of historically permanent elements. They represent essential morphological components that are essential for enabling a relationship of continuity to the historical city, its identity, and its genius loci. On the other hand, we are convinced that we can only reinterpret and reactivate these elements when additional aspects are considered as well, dimensions such as multiplicity, complexity, and contradiction.

At the same time, this work expresses our awareness that scholarship and culture will also play an essential role even in our primarily consumeristic society. For us, imparting knowledge and sharing culture are essential components that positively influence the quality of the architectonic and spatial resources of the city and its ability to further develop the quality of urban life in the future.

Quality and Excellence of the Urban Campus

It is our deeply held conviction that architecture as a discipline should be assigned a high degree of importance because it is capable of improving people's lives. As a unique combination of art and technology, it pursues the goal of fulfilling people's life plans as well as their dreams and their tangible needs. In this regard, the term "campus" is particularly fascinating to us because it represents a location that simultaneously fulfills intellectual as well as emotional concepts of living.

The primary focus of our work is to design and reflect upon the morphology of the architecture and the city. In doing so, it is essential for us to examine how the architectural forms of the city have evolved historically as well as the relationship between the old and the new, between the historical and the modern architecture.

A new and contemporary architecture cannot exist without continuity with the history of the city and of the architecture. We can only explain the development of the city, planning and designing new urban structural forms, as part of a continuous process of metamorphosis. The permanence and the fluctuation of forms must be analyzed, and the morphological rules must be understood so that they can once again be used as tools. We have to investigate and understand everything that the memory, identity, and character of the city has brought forth as heritage from its past, yet we mustn't simply copy it in a formalistic way nor consider them to be silent museum objects.

The Future | Scenarios for the Campus Sites of the Future

2
The School of Athens by Raphael, 1510-1511: Full view and detailed views highlighting the architecture and various groups of figures

As part of this metamorphosis, the "Multiple Campus" will represent a further step in the development of the urban campus, embodying several defining characteristics. However, it will simultaneously open up new, more complex and innovative forms enabling it to be adapted to both present and future conditions and thereby enriching it.

Today, university cities are experiencing exponential growth and are often discussed among specialists as being a model for successful urban development. Just how strongly university cities are growing and continuing to densify can be measured within the context of the broader developments of our current territorial realities and in relationship to other phenomena such as migration. These cities are not just attractive to young people that are looking for a place to study, but also for people who are looking for an urban environment that provides exciting and high-quality living conditions. Synergies develop in various directions, which can lead to diverse and mutually enriching relationships between the university locations (the campus) and the city. These synergies take place on a variety of levels, ranging from the possibility of visiting public events to the shared use of catering and other services.

The high degree of complexity associated with this subject immediately becomes clear when historical, sociological, and technical aspects are considered, and the cultural and geographic factors are not ignored in the process. Therefore, we are deliberately focusing on the urban campus in particular as a physical location that correspondingly interacts with the city in a complex, spatial, and morphological relationship.

The goal of our observations is not to investigate the urban campus historically, sociologically, or economically, but rather morphologically. Our research project is focused on the planning instruments that enable us to conceptualize the urban campus of the future and design it architecturally and in terms of town planning.

In order to demonstrate their excellence, university sites must further strengthen their spatial attractiveness with their architecture and urban design. Especially in a dense city, the need for urban space with a clearly recognizable identity becomes evident. In the compacted city, there is no place for diffuse and indistinct spaces. This matter has little to do with functionality and usage. On the contrary, with urban densification, numerous functions overlap with one another, especially in public spaces. These spaces must be defined by an overarching spatial concept.

In order to investigate the campus as a type of space, to understand its essential nature as a tool in architecture and urban design, we must embark on a quest to find this spatial concept. Once we are capable of recognizing this spatial concept clearly, only then can we use it as a design tool in order to shape the spatial quality in a way that is architecturally appropriate for the urban environment.

Metaphor

As mentioned in previous observations, the Renaissance fresco *The School of Athens* by Raphael[2] represents an excellent artistic metaphor for spatial concept of the "urban campus." In this fresco, we see a location that is clearly defined spatially and partially covered by arches. However, at the same time, it is permeable, meaning that it is characterized by its openings on all sides. It could be the spatial embodiment of an academic thesis or an intellectual statement, which must be clearly formulated and recognizable, yet may not be tautologically closed. Moreover, one must be able to compare it with antitheses to generate a potential synthesis of thoughts, as is common practice in logical/scientific processes as well as for creative and productive research.

The depicted space seems controlled yet at the same time dynamic. It is not static, rather it is open to innovation and progress. It is a space in which intellectuals, artists, and scientists meet and develop a dialogue with one another. Different people gather in small groups. On the one hand, it almost appears to imply a division according to disciplines, reflecting the structure of knowledge. On the other hand, the groups shown here are not closed, but rather open to interdisciplinary connections and reciprocal synergies. It gives rise to the impression that perhaps this picture could be a manifesto for the spatial implementation of cultural exchange within the academic world and set in urban space. At the same time, it reminds us of the ideal concepts of what education and research should mean.

The spatially defining qualities that we recognize in this image come very close to how we understand the concept of the "urban campus."

Threshold

When we look back into the history of cities and consider the first spaces in which human thought was systematized in theories and consider which specific locations in the city helped shape that, we find precise types of structures that were particularly suited for this and embodied this role. In the Greek city, the "stoa" was the construction that spatially embodied a threshold area in which the act of thinking among small groups—within the community of philosophers—came in contact with the public space of the agora. This kind of spatial threshold is a permanent element in the tradition of the campus. Let us consider Thomas Jefferson's arcades at the University of Virginia in Charlottesville. Here the arcades not only form a spatial boundary in the central field (campus), but also act as a "filter" for the more private, interior spaces of teaching and study. This spatial threshold still appears to be an essential component of a campus today.

Typological Variety

There are certain types of buildings that are essential for a city campus, particularly those with ground-floor levels that mediate the relationship to public space, just as they delineate the differences

3
4
5

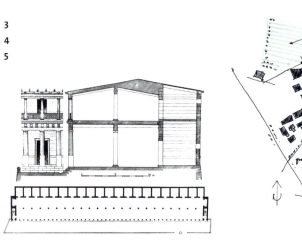

6

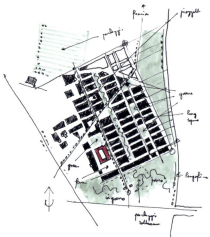

7
8
5

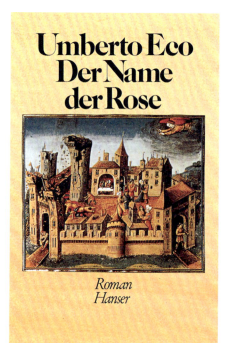

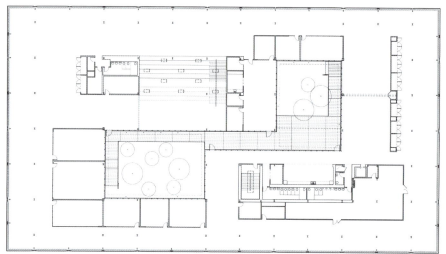

The Future | Scenarios for the Campus Sites of the Future

3
Stoa of Attalos,
2nd century BC

4
Floorplan of the upper level of the Ed Kaplan Family Institute, IIT Chicago

5
Exterior and interior views of the Central Saint Martins campus and Granary Square, London

6
Novartis Campus in Basel: Sketch of the masterplan by Vittorio Magnago Lampugnani

7
Book cover of "The Name of the Rose" by Umberto Eco (German translation)

8
Multifunctional workspace and event room, Faculty of Architecture and the Built Environment, TU Delft

between the private spaces and spaces of presentation and exchange.

At a university, it goes without saying that there are different rooms that require nuanced architectural and typological solutions. Sensitive documents and processes, as well as experiments and preliminary results must be preserved. Lecture halls and presentation spaces, on the other hand, can be used for public events and can be made available to those who are not enrolled in the university as well. Service points and catering areas are spaces on an urban campus that provide the most potential for open exchange with the city.

The architectural and typological differentiation becomes extreme when it is expanded to include institutes in certain natural sciences where the laboratory and research facilities (in halls or warehouses similar to industrial facilities) take on shapes and dimensions that are no longer compatible with the inner-city locations, either for typological or economic reasons.

Typological variety is a further characteristic that represents a constant of the urban campus. From office buildings to residential structures (dormitories or boarding houses), to auditoriums that resemble the typology of theaters, as well as libraries and cafeterias, cafés, and campus shops: there is a wealth of typological solutions that are even found as hybrid combinations. This typological variety evokes the analogy of a "city within the city." Just as in a city, the various buildings and types of structures correspond to hierarchies and structures that enable orientation and identification. From our perspective, all of these things are transformative characters that should be recognized and put to use when designing an urban campus. Furthermore, there are still other topics regarding the urban campus that fascinate us due to their potential to be utilized as tools for design.

Between Preservation and Development

When we think about the university's historical point of origin, interesting associations with libraries emerge. The most important library of antiquity was located in Alexandria. It was a location where contemporary knowledge was collected and preserved in text form, yet it simultaneously served as a meeting point for intellectuals and scholars where rational thought was (further) developed.

In a different historical context, medieval Europe, monasteries were the places charged with the responsibility of preserving and developing culture. In the famous novel The Name of the Rose,[3] despite clearly being a fictional work, Umberto Eco described with great intensity the complex dynamics that developed in medieval monasteries on a scholarly and ethical level. These forces oscillated between respect for the texts, sources, and traditions of the past upon with the disciplines are based, preserving them and passing them on, and, on the other hand, the ethical responsibility or spirit of invention that leads to the further development of the traditional knowledge.

It is precisely this dynamic and this balancing act that defines the campus as a location that spatially embodies the intersection of existing knowledge (in the form of people and sources) and its further development (in the form of education and research). This defining characteristic of the campus should be dealt with as a main theme and should continue to be recognizable in the campus design, even at a time when the development of knowledge is increasingly taking place in virtual form.

The Recognizable Middle: Shaping the Identity and Contemporaneity of the Urban Campus

The location that most closely corresponds to this character and expresses it in its morphology is the central, open space, which seems indispensable as a defining attribute of a campus. From an etymological perspective, the term "campus" is rooted in Latin and means "field." When looking at the spatial typology, early examples of the campus were always characterized by a free field serving as the recognizable midpoint for orientation and helping shape the identity of the site. Thomas Jefferson's University of Virginia in Charlottesville (1825) represents the prototype of this tradition of the academic campus. It can be assumed that this type was produced within a historical and cultural context where neoclassical architecture was seen as a suitable language for embodying a particular ideal of logical and rational planning. Here is the face of a university institution that should serve as an expression of a modern, democratic society. There are several defining factors that influence this image. Among the "French Revolutionary Architecture" as defined by Emil Kaufmann,[4] the works of Claude-Nicolas Ledoux and of Étienne-Louis Boullée absolutely serve as sources of inspiration in this case. In Ledoux's plan for the utopian saltworks in Arc-et-Senans (completed in the year 1779), a central space dominated the industrial facility as an expression of scientifically industrialized production. Boullée's designs for the cenotaph to Newton and for the French National Library (1785), with their almost utopian precision, demonstrate two centrally oriented spaces that are hymns to the work of a great thinker and to the essence of an institution of knowledge.

It is precisely this utopian dimension that defines the "Phalanstère," which was conceived of by the French theorist Charles Fourier (1772-1836). He developed this building, removed from the urban context, as an ideal of a perfect society that would free itself from disruptive external factors by isolating itself and being self-contained. In doing so, it was reminiscent of the comments made by André Corboz on Antolini's project for the Foro Bonaparte in Milan (1801) as being the precursor to the public space of modernity.[5]

However, this self-containment does not in any way belong to the tradition of the urban campus as we know it from the European context, a tradition that expresses fascinating qualities.

9
10
11

12
13

14

The Future | Scenarios for the Campus Sites of the Future

9
Phalanstère, Charles Fourier, 1st half of the 19th century

10
Foro Buonaparte, Giovanni Antonio Antolini, 1801

11
University of Virginia in Charlottesville, Thomas Jefferson, 1826

12
Bibliothèque Nationale, Étienne-Louis Boullée

13
Collegio di Spagna in Bologna

14
Cover of a book by Michel Foucault based on two radio lectures, published in German as: *Die Heterotopien. Der utopische Körper* (Heterotopias. The Utopian Body)

In contrast to the Anglo-Saxon tradition of the campus, there is no spatial delineation of a middle or a middle "free field" separating the urban campus from a "wild," indiscriminate, and hostile landscape (Latin: "ager" or "regio"). The urban campus is not an idyllic place that is concentrated and isolated from the world in order to protect free thinking. The empty space at the center of the urban campus is the location of identity, providing a historical connection as well as recognizability. This central space defined university grounds in Europe long before it did so in Virginia. The University of Bologna, which is the oldest in Europe, was housed in the "Spanish College" (1365/67) during the Middle Ages: one of the first representative buildings to feature a courtyard with arcades, modelled on the design of a monastery with cloisters. The same concept is found at the Sorbonne Université in Paris and the Università della Sapienza in Rome.

Urban Campus as Enclave and Agora

The French linguist Roland Barthes dealt with fundamental questions of structuralist and poststructuralist philosophy. In his book L'empire des signes,[6] he described why the center of a city is the location of truth for Western metaphysics: It is where the values of a civilization are collected and consolidated. Barthes compares this attribute of European culture with that of the Eastern cultures, which, in contrast to the former, are characterized by an empty middle: for example, by a park rather than a dense mass of structures. Following this line of thought, we are interested in the question of whether the morphological middle of a campus, regardless of the dimension and density of this space, does in fact lead to the formation of an identity of knowledge, constantly searching for truth. Fundamentally, the thesis that the central space of a campus inevitably functions as a metaphorical place of identification appears to be validated both by associations and by theoretical literature as well.

The term "campus" reveals a high degree of complexity, even a kind of paradox, and finally a dynamic transformation of its meaning, so that today it is used ever more frequently for various contexts and structural facilities (e.g., "business campus" or "economic campus"). For us, this complexity represents an enrichment, and the increasing complexity represents an adaptation to the demands that a campus has to fulfill in an urban context and will have to fulfill even more so in the future.

At this point, a synthesis is formed between structuralist thoughts that confirm our appreciation of the permanent morphological structures that have developed through history and the poststructuralist approaches that take into consideration the extreme heterogeneity of contemporary culture.

If we think about all of these phenomena, a new potential association with the term "heterotopia" emerges, a term which has already been suggested in the literature and which we can adopt for this purpose.[7] As Michel Foucault used this term in his philosophical discourse, "heterotopias" are spaces or locations that function according to their own rules and embody societal relationships in a special way, in that they represent, negate, or reverse them.[8] They are locations and spaces that correspond with a society, but at the same time, they are uniquely capable of reflecting this society in a different way. We can interpret them as real locations that represent a realization of cultural utopias. Their structures are of a particular type and nature, which is why heterotopias are capable of bringing several spaces that are actually incompatible together within one location and putting them in relation to one another.

Although this fascinating association cannot yet be proven conclusively, it can be used as an inspiring metaphor. Yet if we pursue the association further, it reveals interesting perspectives for reflecting on how we can perceive the urban campus as a kind of microcosm of the city: not only as a city district, but rather as a "city within a city." For our creative design work involving the urban campus, we once again see an endless array of forms emerge with which a city campus can strongly impact urban space.

Even if we do not wish to formulate a conclusive definition of the term "city campus," instead taking a spatial-typological approach to apprehending the essential features of the city campus, it is important for us that some indication of an essential core identity is maintained as a reference point for further design. We are convinced that the essence of the "urban campus" must be discernible as a continuous and constantly alternating layering of "enclave" and "agora."

The first component of this type is the "enclave," a place that presents itself spatially as being clearly defined and legible and appears to a certain extent to be distinctly autonomous within the urban body so that its identity remains discernible. The second component is the "agora," a place that is defined morphologically (in its scale, geometry, its typological and architectonic composition), so as to enable exchange and interaction to take place with all other components of the urban body.

All of the urban design and architectonic elements of the enclave and the agora overlap within the urban campus despite their essential dichotomy, thereby molding it into a heterotopia. One can even propose the hypothesis that the urban campus is gaining an increasing significance as a location of the present that embodies the dichotomy of modern life: a dichotomy between increasingly individualized differentiation between lifestyles on the one hand, and the desire to participate in community life on the other.

However, these elements, the enclave and agora, are clearly recognizable in our discipline as design tools. In planning, they can be used in order to shape the urban campus as a location for study and research within an important cultural institution and to provide excellent opportunities for improving the urban quality of the city.

15
16

17

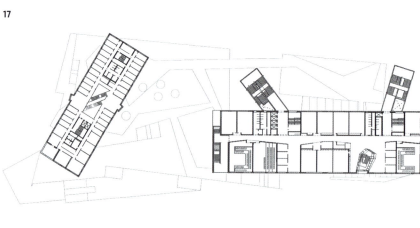

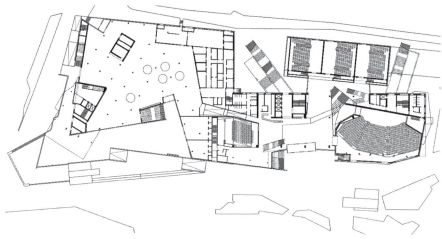

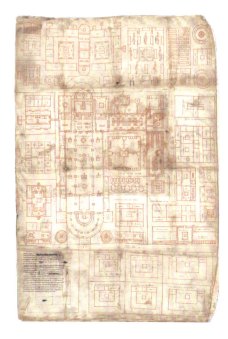

The Future | Scenarios for the Campus Sites of the Future

15
St. Olav Hospital in Trondheim: Site plan and exterior view of a new building

16
Site plan of the Saint Gall Monastery

17
Site plans and exterior view of the BUSarchitektur Teaching Center, Vienna

From Dichotomy to Multiplicity

In our interpretation, the campus is very closely associated with the term "heterotopia" coined by Michel Foucault. The two central components, enclave and agora, which already embody a fascinating dichotomy in themselves, become continuously more complex and meaningful. Going forward, a growing number of spatial dimensions will be necessary in order to fulfill the duties of a campus more efficiently and in a more sophisticated way.

In the future, the spatial expansion of a campus will increasingly take place on both the physical and virtual levels. The virtual dimension is growing along with the inevitable expansion and increasing importance of new forms of media and communication. The academic community is communicating ever more intensively and exchanging information within a scholarly space that acts as an open network. This network functions at a rapid velocity and is constantly undergoing further development.

The actors and the components of a campus function simultaneously on a local and on a global level. The focus of research, data collection, experiments, laboratory methods, and other practices are unfolding ever more frequently on both levels, whether for research or education. For scholars, both are important: the character of the local context on the one hand, and the unlimited potential for communication and exchanging knowledge on the other hand.

Furthermore, spatial diversity manifests itself on a small-scale as well, with different rooms for work, communication, and information exchange. These, in turn, are defined by objects that range from universally standardized products (keyboard, mouse, monitor, etc.) to uniquely personalized aspects that enable individual identities to be recognized. All of these dimensions, the virtual and the physical, the local and the global, the universal and the individual, have to be present simultaneously.

When we consider all these synchronous dimensions of the campus space, we realize that none of them are exclusive nor is any one more important than the other. Instead, there is a growing tendency for all of them to coexist more cohesively and to enrich one another more. That's why it is essential for us at this point of our reflections to include another term from the philosophical discourse of Michel Foucault.

Foucault, and later Gilles Deleuze and Félix Guattari, used the term "multiplicity" (in French: "multiplicité") in order to describe a complex structure that cannot be put in relation to an overarching unit. In our reflections, we interpret and use this philosophical term metaphorically.

Manuel Gausa and Fernando Porras, as well as other authors, have also dealt with the terms "multi" and "multiplicity" in the context of architecture.[9] Here we would not only like to emphasize the etymological root, the Latin adjective "multus" ("many"), but also use this term in a precise way in order to describe the concept of a university urban campus of the future as we envision it.

In essence, our concept of the "Multiple Campus" is a location in which various types of spaces are generated and developed simultaneously. None of these spaces exclusively serve another space, and each space can exist with the others synchronously. All of these different types of spaces can be realized at the same location, shaping it and enlivening it. These spatial types are neither fragments of a whole nor are they in competition with one another, rather, they enrich each other and can benefit from one another, regardless of whether they are virtual or physical spaces. These are types of spaces that not only arise from using architectural types in our designs, but also from being appropriated by the people who use these spaces to manifest their individual visions for their lives.

Developing Urban Quality

While investigating the existing and historical locations of the Universität Hamburg, conducting research on its future campus locations, and exploring their relationship to the city of Hamburg and the world, one important goal for us is to formulate the "Multiple Campus" as a concept for the spatial and architectural resources of the Universität Hamburg in the future.

In this regard, the scope of our observations must also deal with certain essential aspects such as the future of public space in our cities and the role that culture and science play in strengthening urban qualities.

In several different contexts on the continent of Europe, these core ideas presently play an essential role in revitalizing the tradition of the European city and will be essential for renewing the quality of urban spaces in the future. Particularly in Hamburg, these aspects consistently appear to be very strongly connected to the local identity and are thus indispensable components for a vision of the future.

In our culture, public space is increasingly becoming a plane upon which people can engage in a wide variety of activities simultaneously, serving both as a supplement to and an extension of their private spheres. This development is occurring in light of both the increasing diversification and differentiation of individual lifestyles as well as the need to reduce individual living space per capita. In the future, the social, cultural, generational, and ethnic diversity of Hamburg will enable a revitalization of public space, as long as care is taken in the planning to ensure that the public space maintains dynamic flexibility, a defining character, and a distinct identity.

In the future, culture and scholarship will be the core strengths of our society, also in an economic sense, in order to distinguish ourselves among international competition with knowledge and expertise. In Hamburg, the presence of the university can be better linked to the city with new planning measures: Its core functions (research and education) can be represented more efficiently and transparently in public; its centers of competence can take on more intensive forms of knowledge

The Future | Scenarios for the Campus Sites of the Future

18
Student dormitory "Campus Kollegiet" in Odense: Exterior view, floorplan of ground floor, floorplan of dormitory rooms, and view of interior

transfer and information exchange with external partners; its auxiliary functions, such as student residences and other services can be expanded and strengthened.

The fact that scholarship, art, and culture are manifested in public space is evidence of the essential desire to share ideals and aesthetic values with other people. This must be a mandatory requirement for a sustainable city of the future. In Hamburg, more space needs to be found throughout the city for exhibition, event, and informational services, as well as for artworks, installations, performances, actions, events, concerts. These should accompany and supplement the options that are purely oriented toward consumption. This development correlates with a transformation in which the city and public space are no longer perceived as goods to be exploited by people, but rather as creations in which they can take part. In the course of this transition, our society must recognize that land and soil, public space, is not something to be consumed, but rather something that people should actively take part in shaping sustainably.

Strategic Use of Design Tools

At this point, we'd like to reaffirm our conviction that in order to implement this concept, it is necessary to utilize certain strategic planning tools that are equally important both for the Universität Hamburg and for the city. We are even more convinced that the city and the university can only develop harmoniously with one another through synergistic action.

In the foreground, this will primarily involve the development of spatial and morphological designs for distinctly new, qualified, and attractive architecture and urban spaces. These spaces, along with their architectural and typological components, have to consistently make reference to each individual local context, while also making an innovative contribution to future development.

It will also be important to interpret these new spaces as a historic opportunity to take on the tensions of the history, the defining identity, and the existing qualities of the campus, and to project them into a new vision of the future.

In this context, it will be strategically essential to define a timeframe with several stages to realize the project and to differentiate these spaces hierarchically. On the one hand, there are certain indispensable spaces and buildings that should be prioritized and need to be realized quickly. On the other hand, there is a diverse range of proposals that one could consider "open" and remain adaptable to future demands. The primary spaces and structures include the thresholds to the city districts as well as the new entrance situations on Grindelallee for the Von-Melle-Park campus, the Bundesstraße campus, on the Ohnhorststraße in Klein Flottbek, and on Luruper Chaussee for the Science City in Bahrenfeld.

An essential aspect will be structuring the mobility, services, and information in a flexible and dynamic way (while taking into consideration ecological resources and climate), which will primarily be defined by physical and virtual infrastructural elements. In this case, essential infrastructures will include the U5 subway line for the Von-Melle-Park campus and the Bundesstraße campus, as well as the S32 line for the Science City campus in Bahrenfeld.

For this it will be of paramount importance to develop a planning process based on intensive, interdisciplinary cooperation, in order to link the necessary planning expertise with the strategic, political, and economic interests of all of the parties involved.

First and foremost, the types of spaces and structures at the various campus locations need to be planned and implemented more appropriately, taking into consideration the complex goals of research and education. However, at the same time, they should also appear more open and transparent to the outside (in certain areas) in order to enable the transfer of knowledge.

Moreover, the types of spaces and structures that will be present simultaneously in the "Multiple Campus" must be developed with a distinctly elevated level of quality in terms of their composition, design, and materiality.

We are convinced that the measures taken in the context of the "Multiple Campus" will promote the innovative prowess and international competitiveness of UHH scholars and complete the symbiosis between the UHH and the city of Hamburg.

Spatial and Temporal Scale of Implementing the "Multiple Campus"

In the following, we want to present both specifically and paradigmatically how these types of spaces and structures already exist to a certain extent at the UHH campus locations and how they can be created through projects that are being devised at the moment and in the immediate future. In a subsequent step, we will present outlines of projects that will be created on the long term as a further development of the "Multiple Campus" ("The Future"). The four sites—Von-Melle-Park, Bundesstraße, Bahrenfeld, and Klein Flottbek—are very different due to their respective locations, contexts, architectural components, and their free space. At each of these locations, the "Multiple Campus" will emerge, yet the process will be carried out with the help of different solutions in which the individual components are weighted differently.

The University Medical Center Hamburg-Eppendorf (UKE) remains an important site in our minds. Its Future Plan 2050 will be interpreted separately, yet still considered an integrated component of the "Multiple Campus," despite its specificity.

Furthermore, the locations being considered here enable us to represent how the "Multiple Campus" can be implemented at various scales (macro, meso, and micro).

Aside from the ideas outlined here, in order to provide evidence of certain tendencies, we are going

19
21

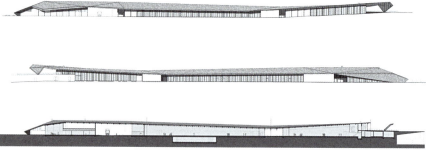

19
20

The Future | Scenarios for the Campus Sites of the Future

19
Swiss Federal Institute of Technology (EPFL) Campus in Lausanne: "Under One Roof" by Kengo Kuma Architects

20
University of Zurich: Courtyard of the main building

21
Spatial atmosphere of a coworking space

to cite several important projects from around the world that either have already been realized or are currently still being planned. These projects make it clear not only that the "Multiple Campus" already exists in some forms, but also that our concepts belong to a brand-new, wide-ranging, international, forward-thinking, and excellent development process at university and non-university campus sites.

Dissolving Territorial Boundaries and Agile Spatial Management

For each of the levels that we are examining, macro, meso, and micro, two phenomena are especially important in order to realize the "Multiple Campus."

The first phenomenon is developing in parallel to the increasing diversity of and differentiation between lifestyles within our society. It has been a long time since people's lives were characterized by a clear separation or differentiation between their work, their residence, and their free time activities. Instead, this kind of separation has dissolved to make way for a kind of "continuum" within which people are constantly reorganizing themselves, determining their own destiny, and shaping their lives creatively. As is often the case, this kind of process develops gradually over time, starting with small groups of pioneers in society. This process will continue to become even more evident in the future due to increasing digitalization and the socio-economic factors associated with it.

Architecture and urban design, as the disciplines bearing the responsibility for shaping living spaces for people, must provide solutions that are appropriate for these current and future lifestyles. The spatial resources have to be utilized so as to achieve the best aesthetic, functional, and economic results with the minimum sensible expenditure.

Along these same lines, the optimal living space of the future will enable itself to be constantly transformed to suit working activities. This is not only true for student dormitories, but also for other residential buildings (for teachers, researchers, employees, and for many other groups of citizens) at the various sites of the "Multiple Campus." Examples that have already been realized in the present show how this kind of flexibility and adaptability can be generated. This development is connected to no small extent to the aforementioned necessity of reducing the residential area per-capita for individuals.

With the "Multiple Campus," the architecture of the buildings designed for work will also provide areas for leisure, rest, and communication at the same time. As we already know from the architectural typology of modern office buildings and workplaces, new and different spatial configurations are constantly being developed in order to fulfill the needs of differentiated working styles and formats dynamically.

Ultimately, this phenomenon of dissolving territorial boundaries is also happening to public space, thereby affecting many types of outdoor spaces on the "Multiple Campus." In our culture, public space is increasingly becoming a level upon which people can develop a wide variety of activities synchronously. It represents both a supplement to and expansion of the sphere of one's private life. This increasing tendency is going to become even stronger, and it does not only concern the users of the university who make use of the campus sites and public spaces, but also the residents and neighbors that do the same.

The phenomenon of dissolving territorial boundaries is connected to a complementary phenomenon that we call "agile spatial management." This term, which we are figuratively appropriating from the innovative business management approach, involves specifically calling into question the hierarchical and consolidated structures of a company. Authors that have dealt with this topic have shown the ways in which the "agile evolution" has emerged as an answer to the increasing complexity of tasks and can be an effective strategy for using resources more efficiently.[10]

In terms of our project, in the "Multiple Campus," new forms of spatial organization and team formation are constantly being developed in order to connect the human and spatial resources more efficiently, creatively, and in a more targeted way. In architecture and urban design, "agile spatial management" fundamentally conforms with the overall strategy of the Universität Hamburg for being a University of Excellence. All of the developments of the university, from research and education to the administration and all overarching strategies (digitalization, communication, internationalization, etc. see table 23, page 26), are consistently being implemented as sub-strategies within this dynamic "agile spatial management."

Macro-Level and Hypertext

Both of these phenomena (dissolving territorial boundaries and agile spatial management) manifest themselves in different ways at each level (macro, meso, and micro), which is something we must research in order to make the "Multiple Campus" a reality.

On the macro-level, we primarily consider the relationship between the campus sites and the total urban body of the Hamburg metropolitan region, as well as the relationship between the "Multiple Campus" and the world. A simple graph (pages 106/107) should demonstrate this concept and clarify in which form the symbiosis between the campus and the city will be implemented at the various levels. This mutually beneficial coexistence emerges as boundaries are dissolved, facilitating flexible accessibility. Mobility infrastructure (such as airports, train stations, railways) can connect places with one another physically, just as places of research and education can become networked throughout the entire world on a virtual level through modern forms of communication. This accessibility is made possible by the partnerships of the UHH, and the collaborations are able to work,

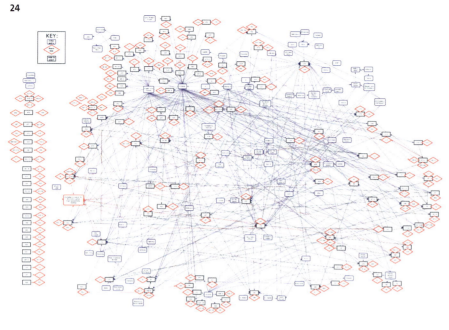

University Development (A)	A1 Concept for Strategic Process and Monitoring	A2 University Development and Governance	A3 Innovation	A4 Basic Participation	A5 Equity and Diversity
Research (B)	B1 Development of Key Fields of Research	B2 Strategy for Excellence (2nd Line of Funding)	B3 Development of Future Researchers	B4 Research Infrastructure	**B5 Cooperation and Knowledge Transfer**
Education (C)	C1 Range of Studies	C2 College-Level Teaching	C3 Transitions in Study Paths, General Studies	C4 Further Education	C5 Training Educators
Administration/ Support (D)	D1 Financing	D2 Future Concept for University Administration	D3 Ensuring and Monitoring Sustainability	D4 Risk Management	D5 Campus Development
Overarching Strategies (E)	E1 Digitalization	**E2 Communication**	**E3 Internationalization**	E4 Quality Management	E5 Legitimation

The Future | Scenarios for the Campus Sites of the Future

22
Simon Rowberry:
Hypertext

23
Overview of the strategies and partial strategies for the future development of the Universität Hamburg, highlighting the most important aspects for the Multiple Campus strategy

24
Atlassian headquarters in San Francisco

25
The Archimedes Palimpsest

conversely, because Hamburg's partners are easily accessible physically and virtually.

The development of transportation options (such as the planned U5 subway line) and the digitalization process are going to intensify this accessibility and become fundamental components of a hypertextual structure of the "Multiple Campus."

In this context, we are specifically using the term "hypertext" as a metaphor. "Hypertext" is an electronic document that collects several texts. A classic, traditional anthology consists of a series of texts. In contrast to that, the "hypertext" is a system in which the links between the text are more important that the texts themselves, and in which the texts can continually be reorganized according to new rules. In the future, the UHH "Multiple Campus" will continue to become even more of a constituent of this "hypertext" as territorial boundaries and distances become relativized and as new agile links continue to emerge.

Meso-Level and Palimpsest

There is one important metaphor that we would like to use for our further discussion of the meso-level, that of the "palimpsest."

André Corboz uses the metaphor of the "palimpsest" in order to describe the territory as a system of layers where a series of overlapping signs and networks alternate over the course of time.[11] Morphological signs and physical traces from various eras accumulate at one location, defining the character and the memory of this space as the result of a synthesis of these moments.

If we consider this metaphor from a design perspective, it becomes clear that by implementing targeted measures and by utilizing specific tools, we can shape urban spaces as palimpsests in which several different events can play out alternatingly or synchronously. These planning tools will enable these locations to function as defining exterior spaces of the "Multiple Campus" on the one hand, and as morphological thresholds between the campus site and the urban environment on the other. This is where the campus and urban space develop symbiotically and evolve synchronously.

These transitional zones are recognizable not only as integrative areas of the urban campus, but also as a visible unit (according to our term the "enclave") and as essential public spaces in the urban context (according to our term "agora"). These kinds of transit zones exist already to some extent, primarily at the Von-Melle-Park campus. Two squares, Allende-Platz and Joseph-Carlebach-Platz, where events such as flea markets and the festival of cultures take place, are not only integrative gateway areas to the university campus, but also locations of extreme urban intensity. The new gateway areas on Moorweidenstraße and Schlüterstraße around the "Studierendenwerk" building will also be designed with this characteristic. There are excellent opportunities to allow these kinds of locations to emerge, such as the fascinating idea of creating a passage with a learning center between Moorweidenstraße and the "Studierendenwerk" building, or a passage with an exhibition space (in the glass-roofed courtyard of the "Alten Pferdestall") between Allende-Platz and Grindelallee.

The clearest example of such a palimpsest will be Grindelallee, which will develop into the "Campus Boulevard." By linking the Von-Melle-Park campus with the Bundesstraße campus, the boulevard will emerge as an integral part of the campus while simultaneously becoming consolidated into the urban environment as a city avenue. With the implementation of the U5 subway line and the university subway station, Grindelallee will develop into a place of mobility and accessibility. With exhibition spaces, open workshops (the scholastic workshop or scholastic research center), and museum structures (Museum of Natural History, or "Evolutioneum"), Grindelallee will become a space for presentation, communication, and knowledge transfer.

By further developing the existing cultural, athletic, and leisure functions, as well as food services and retail (as shown on our "treasure map"), and supported by the intermodal mobility, Grindelallee will become a kind of "mall": a space for the flaneur to saunter, a place of leisure and communication. These multiple types of space will overlap and all exist at the same location simultaneously.

The new "Futurium" in Berlin is indicative of analog tendencies and strategies in the field of knowledge transfer. It represents one possibility for using space simultaneously as a stage, museum, laboratory, and forum for communication between science and society.

As planned with the MIND project in Milan, an "Innovation District" will emerge here (in the Science City Bahrenfeld) as an ecosystem in which the experimental forms of research will be combined with a "Living Lab" in order to promote social and cultural innovation. An additional advantage in Hamburg is that this ecosystem will be developed both in the heart of the historic city center as well as in a newly planned district.

The campus location in Klein Flottbek can provide a special form of "Multiple Campus" and its own form of urbanity when its focus on biodiversity is developed.

In this case as well, the contextual link can be strengthened by targeted measures, such as structural consolidation in the Ohnhorststraße area and the train station, as well as by implementing the mobility of the S-Bahn train line, bus routes, bike paths, and walkways. The consolidation can provide spaces and infrastructures for a center of biodiversity while at the same time facilitating a link between the botanical garden and areas for living, working, researching, and exhibiting, along with natural mobility and further green spaces.

One can draw clear analogies here with campus tendencies at other institutions such as the EPFL Lausanne and IIT Chicago, which are characterized by green spaces and mobility. The botanical garden should be seen as a special form of urban space, as

26

27
28
29

The Future | Scenarios for the Campus Sites of the Future

26
Exterior and interior views of the Futurium in Berlin, by Richter Musikowski Architekten

27
View of the Palmaille avenue in Hamburg-Altona

28
MIND Milano Innovation District – Mobility

29
MIND Milano Innovation District – Public Space

a city park. In this sense, the "Multiple Campus" can emerge as a palimpsest of campus and city here as well, of course with the help of certain morphological designs.

With the Future Plan 2050, the UKE premises will be further developed into an area that can be characterized as a "Health Park." At this site, not only will the various clinics of the UKE and their research facilities and services be tightly interwoven with one another, but also with the facilities of external cooperation partners in the health sector.

Furthermore, it will experience yet another transformation to become an open "city in the city" with medical facilities, services, retail, food services, zones of passage and of rest, which will also be open to people from the surrounding districts. Mobility will play a central role in this case as well. On the long-term, there will be a UKE subway station on the planned U5 line.

For the "Multiple Campus," the time spent at the UKE by the patients, the night-shift personnel, as well as the retail and food services can be seen as a special form of "temporary residence" and as incipient cores of urbanity. These cores of urbanity have also been realized at St. Olavs Hospital in Trondheim, for example, and can serve as a reference point for future endeavors to strengthen the cooperation between the UKE and the urban environment.

Three Supplementary Factors for Two Main Sites

Going forward, the strongly connected campus sites of Von-Melle-Park, Bundesstraße, and Science City Bahrenfeld will be the most important and primary locations of the university. The crucial factors that will enable the "Multiple Campus" to be realized at these sites are innovative forms of residential construction, new building types for urban commerce and production, and mobility.

First of all, the types of residential structures built for students will provide innovative forms of living, not just for students who are already employed, but also for those who live there with their family or are raising children on their own. As it has become clear from several examples of contemporary tendencies, differentiated forms of "co-living" and "co-working," temporary housing, and housing with auxiliary services are being provided more and more frequently.

Along the "Campus Boulevard" and in the new Science City in Bahrenfeld, different types of buildings for urban business and urban production will be realized, also in cooperation with private companies. In these buildings, a wide spectrum of new businesses (from start-ups to micro-factories) will be developed, activating important synergies with university research in the field of innovation.

The third critical factor concerns innovative mobility. As much as possible, car-free zones should be created so as to prioritize pedestrians and cyclists. Aside from increasing the global and national accessibility (with public transportation connections to the main train station and the airport), there will be an intelligent mobility infrastructure with a wide range of uninterrupted, sustainable mobility services (autonomous driving and vehicle sharing). This innovative mobility will enable sustainability and efficiency to constitute two additional defining characteristics of the "Multiple Campus."

In the literature on this topic, transdisciplinary and participative work are discussed as an essential part of a living laboratory in which academia and society are directly connected to one another.[12] On the long term, living laboratories should help solve the complex challenges involved in coupling scholarly language with the vernacular.

With the realization of these projects, scientific research and forward-thinking scholarship conducted at Universities of Excellence will not be perceived by politicians and the general public as a financial "burden," but rather as defining aspects of their existence.

As previously mentioned in the formulation of the term "Multiple Campus," each of these spaces will coexist adjacent to the other at the same time and equal in value. Different types of spaces will be realized in order to shape, enliven, and define the same location. There will not be any competition emerging between these spaces, which can simultaneously be both virtual and physical in nature. On the contrary, they will enrich one another and develop synergies in order to profit from each other and generate excellent spatial quality.

Micro-Level and Multispace

On the micro-level, the role of architectural typology and composition will be of primary importance. On this level, some of the existing buildings will of course retain their qualities and still remain icons of the history of the UHH that shape its identity. Special structures, such as the main building or the Audimax by Bernhard Hermkes in Von-Melle-Park, will function as reference points for developing the locations of the "Multiple Campus."

Analogously, certain types of spaces, such as cubicle offices, open-plan offices, or lecture halls, are indispensable and will continue to be used in order to fulfill certain important tasks in research and education.

Lecture halls and libraries are among the structures that define the identity of the campus; these spaces embody the identity of the university. They are places where the transfer of knowledge, communication, reflection, and thought take place institutionally. As such, they are integral to the identity and the memory of the university and will be kept as permanent fixtures.

Surely these types of spaces will be retrofitted with new technical equipment so they can fulfill the requirements that come along with the new dimensions of research and learning in the digital era. This adaption is made possible because the users integrate themselves into the physical and virtual network of the global academic community and can participate in this community.

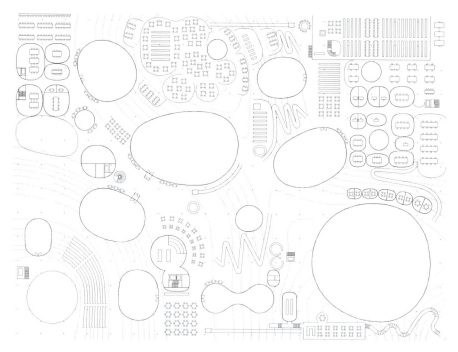

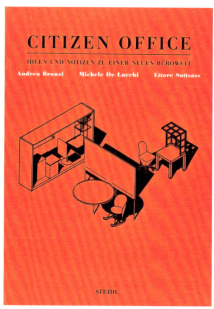

The Future | Scenarios for the Campus Sites of the Future

30
Exterior view of the courtyard of the Tietgen Residence Hall in Copenhagen

31
Rolex Learning Center, Swiss Federal Institute of Technology (EPFL) Campus in Lausanne: floorplan and view of exterior

32
Book cover: *Citizen Office.* Andrea Branzi. Michele De Lucchi. Ettore Sottsass, Alexander von Vegesack (Ed.)

However, in the future, there will be a stronger emphasis on finding innovative solutions for planning and constructing architecture that is best capable of fulfilling the complex demands of the tasks at hand (especially in the field of research). This is not only an important topic for university structures designed for research and education but is also part of a global phenomenon that incorporates various working environments into our contemporary society.

In the 1990s, a few perceptive architects and authors analyzed the transformation of workplaces in the post-industrial society and posed the question of how the workplaces of the future will be designed and what their quality standards will be.[13]

Not only did they consider the rapid and radical changes in working processes, but many of the aspects resulting from this as well, such as communication processes, interactions that occur over the course of projects carried out together by various teams or groups. In particular, the office as a location of complex relationships and as an essential component of life in our society, "creates a dynamic in itself, bringing about actions, demands, and desires that go far beyond what the office as a workspace normally seems to define."[14]

Two aspects are important for us at this point. First, the colleagues who observed this dynamic development were designers (like us) and therefore immediately dealt with the tools that are able to specify the spatial and architectural design of these working locations. Second, the analytical, theoretical, and conceptual work displays a pioneering character in the context of a transition that is actually taking place in our society and in the discipline of architecture.

In recent years, there has been an increase in scholarly literature dealing with these changes and investigating the synergies between the spatial design of workplaces, efficiency, creativity, and excellence in various forms of work.[15] In theoretical reflections and in planning, investigations are being conducted on which innovative spatial designs and solutions, along with digitalization, can lead to new dimensions of work. Hybrid types of spaces and structures that can provide a large bandwidth of spatial options, either simultaneously or alternatively, are being investigated and implemented. Aside from conventional solutions, there is also an increasing number of alternative forms of open and non-territorial office concepts designed to promote flexibility, openness, and transparency being put into effect. This primarily applies to two kinds of companies: those in the IT sector and for start-ups.

In the IT sector, the concrete, physical design of the working space has to be in harmony with the abstract, virtual dimension. For start-ups, great synergies for the working processes have to be developed using a minimal number of resources, and they constantly have to be reinvented and redesigned. For these companies, innovative research and a substantial need for knowledge-transfer play a central role, so they are very closely related to university facilities for research and education. For the "Multiple Campus" of the future, new types of spaces and structures will be essential for shaping these forms of innovative research and knowledge transfer.

By now, even more conventional and institutionalized businesses (e.g., in the automotive industry) have come to the realization that they have to adapt to new challenges (such as e-mobility) at a rapid pace. As a result, they are transforming their structures more towards "agile management," both in terms of personnel and spatial resources. Concepts such as "co-working" and "co-living" spaces have become established topics in architecture, both in theoretical reflections and in practice.

For a while now, buildings as places for knowledge transfer and for agile research and learning processes have been emerging at innovative university campus sites, such as the renowned "Learning Center" at the EPFL in Lausanne. The planned Lecture Hall Center at the UHH Bahrenfeld campus will represent a similar space. Many further typologically innovative and hybrid structures and spaces are being conceived of at the moment and will be built in the coming years. These will expand on the existing typological spectrum, such as the Loki Schmidt Museum in the Botanical Garden Flottbek, the observatory in Bergedorf, the sports park on Rothenbaumchaussee, or the greenhouses by Hermkes in the Planten un Blomen park, which are open to schools and associations, as well as to the public.

Three Strategies for Potential Scenarios

In order to put our theoretical considerations to the test and to be able to give them a preliminary shape, we have developed design scenarios that will be presented here. The goal is to apply our methodological ideas with examples for three locations: at Von-Melle-Park, on Bundesstraße, and in Klein Flottbek. However, these scenarios are not indicative of finished projects, but rather they provide reference points for the discussions that will be had among everyone involved in planning the future of these campus sites.

In the first step, we define three fundamental categories of spaces:
- Spaces for external functions (living, working, dining, and services) or university functions relating to the public
- Spaces for shared usage that are available to residents, visitors, and university members alike, "sharing spaces"
- Spaces that are available to the students and university staff exclusively, so pure academic education can take place and sensitive research can be conducted.

We are convinced that different strategies can be applied in order to achieve multiplicity in the urban morphological fabric and architectural typology.

In the second step, we have tested three strategies that have been given the working titles "Layers," "Mosaic," and "Strata." These can be described as follows:

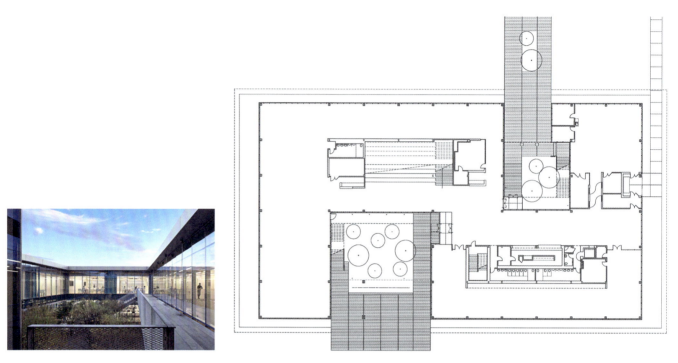

The Future | Scenarios for the Campus Sites of the Future

Ed Kaplan Family Institute by John Ronan, Chicago IIT Main Campus: Courtyard view, floorplan of ground floor, and view of exterior

Layers: With this strategy, all of the ground floors and all of the areas that are located near urban public space will be designated primarily for external functions related to the general public. In the area above that, open working spaces, atria, and foyers should enable "sharing spaces." Finally, on the upper floors, academic learning and research activities can take place exclusively and privately.

This strategy is based on a vertical differentiation of the university spaces in fundamentally hybrid types of structures, creating a visual metaphor for different urban levels.

Mosaic: This strategy works explicitly with the concept of the fragment. Architectural and spatial types are differentiated and specifically developed in order to fulfill their individual purpose in an ideal way: areas concerning the public, sharing spaces, and spaces purely for academic research and scholarship. This strategy creates an archipelago of spaces and buildings that are typologically differentiated, producing a diverse morphological image through juxtapositions and contrast.

Strata: This strategy is defined by precise differentiation between types of spaces and architecture. As in the previous strategy, these spaces will be specifically developed in order to ideally fulfil their individual purpose: areas concerning the public, sharing spaces, and spaces purely for academic research and scholarship. This strategy organizes spaces and structures in linear arrangements that we call "strata." These strata enable us to progressively transition between the maximum degree of concentration of public functions at the periphery of the campus and the maximum degree of pure scholarship and sensitive academic research in the interior of the campus. All of the other areas can be found in between, primarily enabling "sharing spaces" to emerge. This strategy enables different parts of the campus to be distinctly characterized while simultaneously promoting a kind of horizontal osmotic continuity between the city and the cores of the campus sites.

Using these different strategies turns architecture and the urban morphological fabric into an expression of multiplicity and regulates access to various spaces and resources.

From "Common Space" to "Multiple Campus"

In the future of the "Multiple Campus," indoor and outdoor spaces as well as UHH buildings will increasingly provide co-working and co-living spaces for residents, partners, and entrepreneurs from neighboring districts. The concept of the "Multiple Campus" further develops the idea of "common space" as a turn in the collective perception of spaces of interaction in our culture. The "Multiple Campus" will be a permanent impulse for elevating the quality of the university and the city to an equal extent.

The transfer of knowledge between all social groups and age groups will be broadened and become a defining aspect of excellence at the UHH. The Universität Hamburg will become an even more strongly integrated and indispensable aspect of the urban environment in the city of Hamburg and its global perception and impact.

This transition and the completion of this metamorphosis will even provide the Universität Hamburg with the opportunity not only to bolster its existing strengths in its areas of expertise, but where necessary, also to break out of the conventional disciplinary framework by achieving interdisciplinarity and transdisciplinarity. By consolidating its permanent structures and redesigning its profile, expertise, and knowledge transfer to embrace flexibility and agility, the university will be able to optimally adapt to the dynamically developing challenges of the future.

The "Multiple Campus" will promote the innovative capabilities and international competitiveness of UHH scholars, while simultaneously strengthening the symbiosis between the UHH and the city of Hamburg, thus achieving architectural and urban excellence not just on a local level, but on a global level as well. (PF)

34

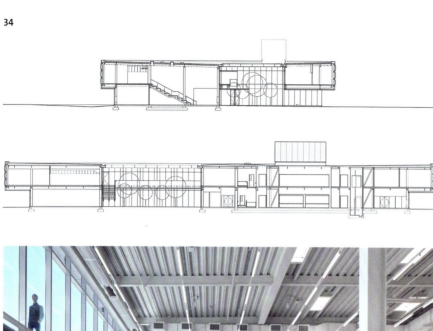

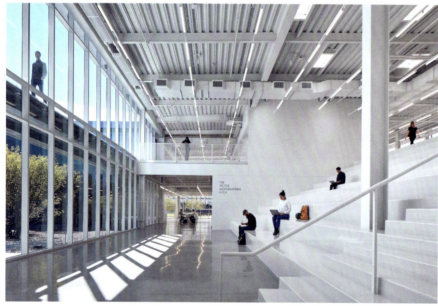

35
36
37

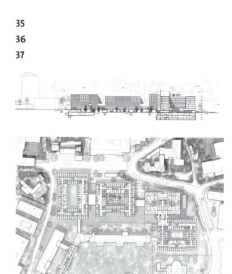

The Future | Scenarios for the Campus Sites of the Future

34
Ed Kaplan Family Institute by John Ronan, Chicago IIT Main Campus: Cross-section and views of interior

35
USZ Zürich Kernareal, cross-section and site plan

36
S.R. Crown Hall by Ludwig Mies van der Rohe, Chicago IIT Main Campus

37
Columbia University Manhattanville Campus in New York City: The Forum, cross-section and campus view from the south

1 Paolo Fusi, Stadtcampus: Zwischen Enklave und Agora (Urban Campus: Between Enclave and Agora), Lehrstuhl Städtebaulicher Entwurf – Urban Design, HCU. Hamburg 2016. **2** Raffael Sanzio, La scuola di Atene (The School of Athens), 1510/11, Fresco, Stanza della Segnatura, The Vatican.
3 Umberto Eco, Il nome della rosa (The Name of the Rose), Bompiani 1980. **4** Emil Kaufmann, "Three Revolutionary Architects: Boullée, Ledoux, Lequeu", in: Transactions of the American Philosophical Society, Philadelphia 1952. **5** André Corboz, "Auf der Suche nach 'dem' Raum" (Searching for "the" Space), in: Die Kunst, Stadt und Land zum Sprechen zu bringen, Bauwelt Fundamente 123, Birkhäuser, Basle/Berlin/Boston 2001.
6 Roland Barthes, L'empire des signes (The Empire of Signs), Skira, Paris 1970. **7** Andrea Deplazes, "The Campus as Location and Strategy: Thumbnail Sketches of Science City", in: Campus and the City: Urban Design for the Knowledge Society, eds. v. K. Höger and K. Christiaanse, gta, Zurich 2007. **8** cf. "Eterotopie" (Heterotopia), in: Archivio Foucault, Feltrinelli, Milan 1998. **9** Cros, Susanna (Ed.): *The Metapolis Dictionary of Advanced Architecture: City, Technology and Society in the Information Age*. Actar, Barcelona, 2003
10 Marko Lasnia, Valentin Nowotny, Agile Evolution – aktiv, effizient, kommunikativ: Eine Anleitung zur agilen Transformation (Agile Evolution – Active, Efficient, Communicative: A Manual for Agile Transformations), Business Village GmbH, Göttingen 2018. **11** André Corboz, "Das Territorium als Palimpsest" (Territory as Palimpsest), in: Die Kunst, Stadt und Land zum Sprechen zu bringen, Bauwelt Fundamente 123, Birkhäuser, Basle/Berlin/Boston 2001. **12** Oliver Parodi, "Reallabor im Quartier" (Living Laboratory in the Quarter), in: CoLiving Campus, eds. v. Uwe Brederlau, Johannes-Göderitz-Preis 2018, TU Braunschweig, Institut für Städtebau und Entwurfsmethodik, Braunschweig 2018. **13** Uta Brandes, "Das Veralten des Büros" (The Aging of the Office), in: Alexander von Vegesack (Ed.), Citizen Office: Ideen und Notizen zu einer neuen Bürowelt, Steidl, Göttingen 1994, p. 26.
14 Parodi, 2018, (see footnote 12), p. 26. **15** Cf. Dark Horse Innovation, New Workspace Playbook: Taktiken, Strategien, Spielzüge (New Workspace Playbook: Tactics, Strategies, Plays), Murmann, Hamburg 2018; Thomas Wagner, "Willkommen im Multispace: Weniger Hierarchie, mehr Spaß?" (Welcome to the Multispace: Less Hierarchy, More Fun?), in: Detail Inside 02/18, Detail Business Information GmbH, Munich 2018; Jelena Altmann, "Platz für alle" (Space for Everyone), in: impulse 11/2018, Impulse Medien GmbH, Berlin 2018.

The Universität Hamburg of the Future

Scenario Designs and Future Plans for the Main Sites

Having presented the theoretical approach, which conceives of the university locations according to the principle of a Multiple Campus, and having described the basic concept thereof, now the scenarios for the future of the Universität Hamburg will be shown in the form of plans and axonometric views. The scenarios presented here are to be understood as idealized applications of the conceptual themes of a Multiple Campus, and do not represent finalized plans for the individual sites.

Furthermore, this approach is limited to the following locations: Von-Melle-Park, Bundesstraße, and Klein Flottbek. In this context, the Science City Bahrenfeld and the University Medical Center Hamburg-Eppendorf will not be taken into consideration, because clearly defined scenarios for the future of these sites have concurrently emerged from other projects, which also contain many important aspects of a Multiple Campus on their own.

The historical campus at Von-Melle-Park will have to take particularly large steps in order to achieve the long-term vision for the future. By fundamentally restructuring the urban relationship between the interior of the campus and main avenue, Grindelallee, two major changes will occur. The campus interior will be more strongly defined, while at the same time, a relationship to the new "campus boulevard" will be generated with the redesign of Grindelallee.

In the second decade of the 21st century, an overarching vision for the Bundesstraße Campus was already developed, however, since then, the underlying parameters regarding the usage of that site have changed dramatically. Therefore, it is worth thinking past these existing plans and reconceiving the basic urban design for this site as well. This manifests itself both in a strengthened orientation toward Grindelallee, which will become the new central axis of the combined urban campus of Von-Melle-Park and Bundesstraße, and in a connection to the important public transportation hub, the subway station Schlump, where there will be a new campus entrance area.

In the vision presented here, the Klein Flottbek Campus will play a long-term role as the Center for Biodiversity, and fitting to this role, it will encompass a diverse range of uses and offerings to supplement the university's research and educational spectrum, despite the planned relocation of the central functions of the Biology department to Bahrenfeld. The most important gesture in terms of the urban design here is the consolidation along the rapid transit line parallel to Ohnhorststraße, which will then also be integrated into the campus.

For each of these three locations—or two, considering that Von-Melle-Park and Bundesstraße will merge into one Urban Campus—three different design scenarios have been developed according to these overarching principles: "Layers," "Mosaic," and "Strata." In the following, these will be described in connection with the visual representations of the individual campus sites.

The long-term visions for the Science City Bahrenfeld and for the University Medical Center Hamburg-Eppendorf will be described in this chapter according to the current plans and concepts for these sites. The concept for the Science City Bahrenfeld, which was published in 2019, will be presented here as well. For the University Medical Center Hamburg-Eppendorf, the "Future Plan 2050" will be described. (PF/JB)

The Urban Campus:
Von-Melle-Park & Bundesstraße

Layers – Mosaic – Strata

In the future vision of the Universität Hamburg, the campus sites Von-Melle-Park and Bundesstraße will be regarded as one coherent Urban Campus. Grindelallee will serve as the hinge connecting these two areas, and it will be redesigned to become the Campus Boulevard. After the planned subway line is completed, the bus lanes can be removed, and the street space can be repartitioned with broad walkways to provide it with the atmosphere of a boulevard. The existing campus buildings on this axis and those yet to be constructed will be designed with the aim of optimizing the visibility of the university from this street, and the connecting pathways between the two sections of this campus will be improved.

Layers

In this scenario, the historic straight line between the current Allende-Platz and the southern part of Schlüterstraße is revisited, as it runs parallel to Grindelallee, and it is reshaped as a boundary to the consolidated structural development between these two outer edges. Aside from the historic building of the University Library (Staats- und Universitätsbibliothek), also known as the "horse stable," a new developmental design with interrupted block structures is created that spans from the corner of Moorweidenstraße to the corner of Grindelhof. At the southeastern end, the library's newer structure, as a cuboid polygon, intermediates between the direction of the new library passage and the structures that are aligned to Grindelallee at right angles. At the northwestern end, the block containing the Grindelhof development, Pferdestall, and the new cultural passage is enclosed with one large gesture and provided with a high point that complements the Philosophers Tower and the newly built Student Center, turning them into a triad. Here, the passageway to the campus interior is distinctly turned clockwise from the orthogonal lines to Grindelallee, in order to indicate their function as the connection to the Bundesstraße section of the Urban Campus. In between these two endpoints, an interrupted row of structures is developed along Grindelallee, and U-shaped and E-shaped structures behind them in the campus interior. Within all of the buildings in this scenario, the functions overlap vertically according to the Layers principle, with the ground floors serving as public spaces and the upper levels exclusively for the university.

In the Bundesstraße section of the Urban Campus, new supplementary structures are envisaged for the area near the Schlump subway station. In the Layers scenario, the vertical form of the mixed-functionality buildings is derived from the layout of the streets and the lines provided by the other newly developed structures of the campus. In between the Schröderstift building and the street Beim Schlump, a new line of buildings is developed, expanding the large block-perimeter development of the Haus der Erde to the intersection where the subway station is located. The present-day flat-roofed structures of the station is replaced by a structure with distinctive massing that is oriented toward the Schäferkampsallee side. Two additional cubic structures emerge on Schröderstiftstraße in the second row, behind the two outer wings of the Schröderstift development and between the Geomatikum and the street Schröderstiftsweg.

Mosaic

In this scenario, the new structures are shaped like polygonal mosaic stones, and the distinction between external and internal usage does not occur

38
Universität Hamburg Urban Campus, Von-Melle-Park and Bundesstraße: Spatial structures and interconnections

on the vertical axis, but rather according to the buildings on the whole. So, each mosaic piece possesses its own specific function in its entirety. The Audimax, despite being originally planned by Seitz as an independent and solitary structure and kept that way in the other scenarios, is intentionally seen as a piece of the mosaic structure here. This way, just like the adjacent new structures, it takes on the role as a boundary to the free space within the campus, which is thus also reduced overall and enclosed on the southeast side. This scenario envisions a reconstructed Studierendenwerk that becomes part of this mosaic landscape just like all of the other structures from Seitz's concept. At the same time, secondary campus spaces are created by the free spaces within the new design, which, similar to the concept for the Bundesstraße campus, are arranged at various positions between the interior and exterior of the campus, some serving as courtyards, others as openings to the primary campus space or to the outer edges of the campus. In this case as well, a distinct solitary structure next to the Pferdestall is created as a high point for the campus.

In the area of the Schröderstift and the Schlump station, polygonal volumes with specific uses are created. In contrast to the constellation of four new structures in the Layers scenario, here the development is broken down into a larger number of individual buildings, for example at Schlump station. Even the courtyard of the Schröderstift is provided with two additional polygonal structures aligned at oblique angles, standing in contrast to the perpendicularity of the Schröderstift. Further individual buildings at the street corner of Beim Schlump and Schröderstraße, next to the Haus der Erde on Beim Schlump, and in between the Geomatikum, Haus der Erde, and the developments on Schröderstiftweg.

Strata

The straight line between Allende-Platz and Schlüterstraße to the south is reestablished in this scenario as well, albeit partially interrupted in the vicinity of the library in order to create a new plaza situation facing the reconstructed Studierendenwerk. The rows of structures with slight protrusions and recesses between Grindelallee and the campus interior are conceived of as three parallel strata. The distribution of usage, ranging from external to internal, is arranged with each row of buildings as one stratum, from the outer row facing the campus boulevard, Grindelallee, passing through a middle zone to the interior part of the campus. Due to the density of the developments in the Strata scenario, it maintains the character of larger block units, especially in contrast to the large entryway between the campus interior and Grindelallee on the west side of the campus. In this scenario, there is also the triad of high points with the reconstructed Studierendenwerk, the Philosophers Tower, and the new building at the Pferdestall.

In this scenario, there is once again a close relationship to the Layers variant in terms of how the structural volumes are shaped, whereas in this case, the usage is defined for entire buildings. The public stratum is aligned with the axes running through Schäferkampsallee and Schröderstiftstraße, oriented toward these two streets, only to be broken up by the wings of the Schröderstift. An additional stratum, which has a usage positioned in between public and private, arises as a new bar-shaped structure positioned at a slightly oblique angle behind the main building of the Schröderstift and separated at the upper floors.

In the following pages, these three scenarios for the Urban Campus are presented visually. (PF/JB)

- Core spaces
- Liminal spaces
- Internal structures
- Primary connections
- Ancillary connections

39
Urban Campus,
Von-Melle-Park and
Bundesstraße: Site plan
for the Layers Scenario

40
Urban Campus,
Von-Melle-Park and
Bundesstraße: Site plan
for the Mosaic Scenario

41
Urban Campus,
Von-Melle-Park and
Bundesstraße: Site plan
for the Strata Scenario

- Public
- Semi-public
- Ground floor public, upper floors semi-public
- Internal spaces
- Ground floor public, upper floors internal

42
Urban Campus, Von-Melle-Park and Bundesstraße: Structures and outdoor spaces, Layers Scenario, M 1:10,000

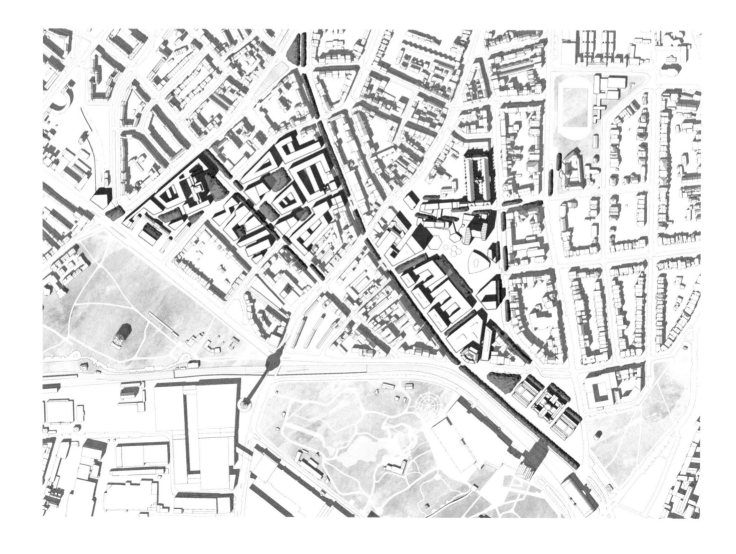

43
Urban Campus,
Von-Melle-Park and
Bundesstraße: 3D model,
Layers Scenario

44
Urban Campus, Von-Melle-Park and Bundesstraße: Axonometric view of Layers Scenario

The Future | The Urban Campus: Von-Melle-Park & Bundesstraße

45
Von-Melle-Park: Visualization with functional areas of Layers Scenario

■ Public
■ Semi-public
■ Internal spaces

The Future | The Urban Campus: Von-Melle-Park & Bundesstraße

46
Von-Melle-Park: 3D model of Layers Scenario, views from four different directions

47
Bundesstraße: Visualization of Layers Scenario with functional areas

The Future | The Urban Campus: Von-Melle-Park & Bundesstraße

48
Bundesstraße: 3D model, Layers Scenario, views from four different directions

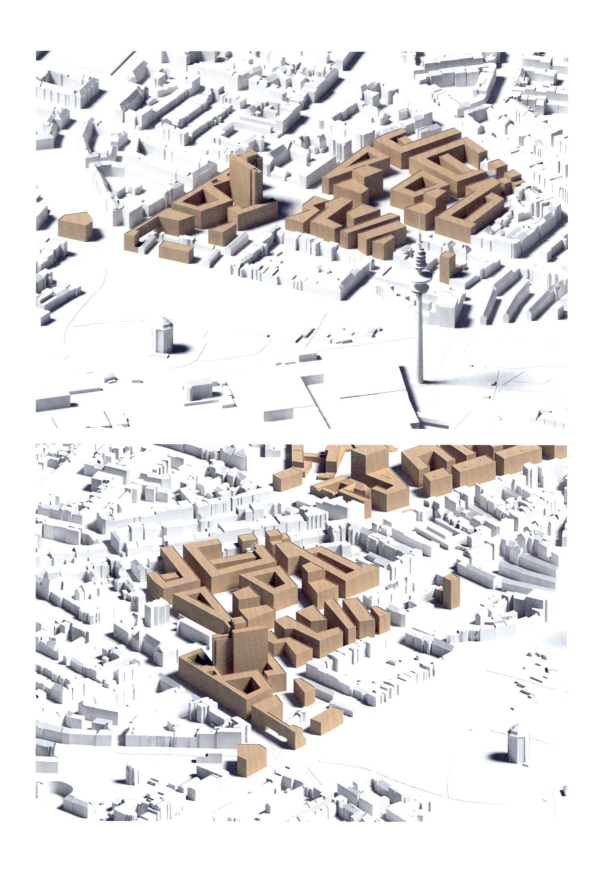

49
Urban Campus,
Von-Melle-Park and
Bundesstraße: Structures
and outdoor spaces,
Mosaic Scenario,
M 1:10,000

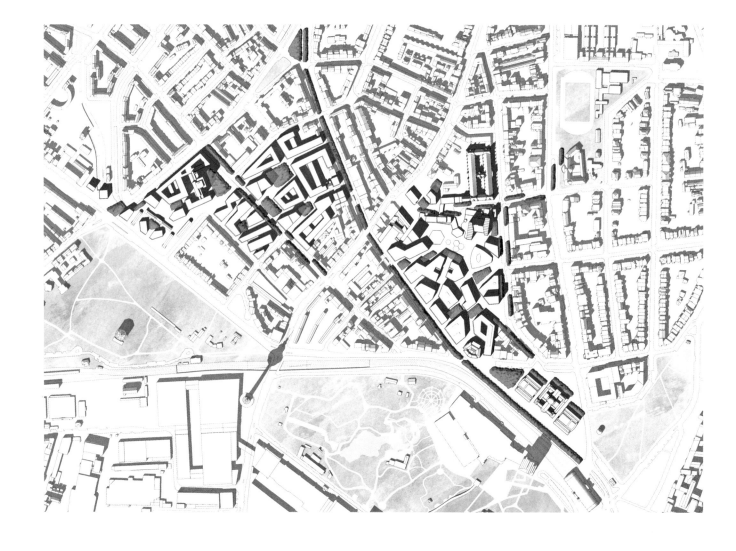

50
Urban Campus,
Von-Melle-Park and
Bundesstraße: 3D model,
Mosaic Scenario

51
Urban Campus, Von-Melle-Park and Bundesstraße: Axonometric view of Mosaic Scenario

52
Von-Melle-Park: Visualization with functional areas of Mosaic Scenario

■ Public
■ Semi-public
■ Internal spaces

The Future | The Urban Campus: Von-Melle-Park & Bundesstraße

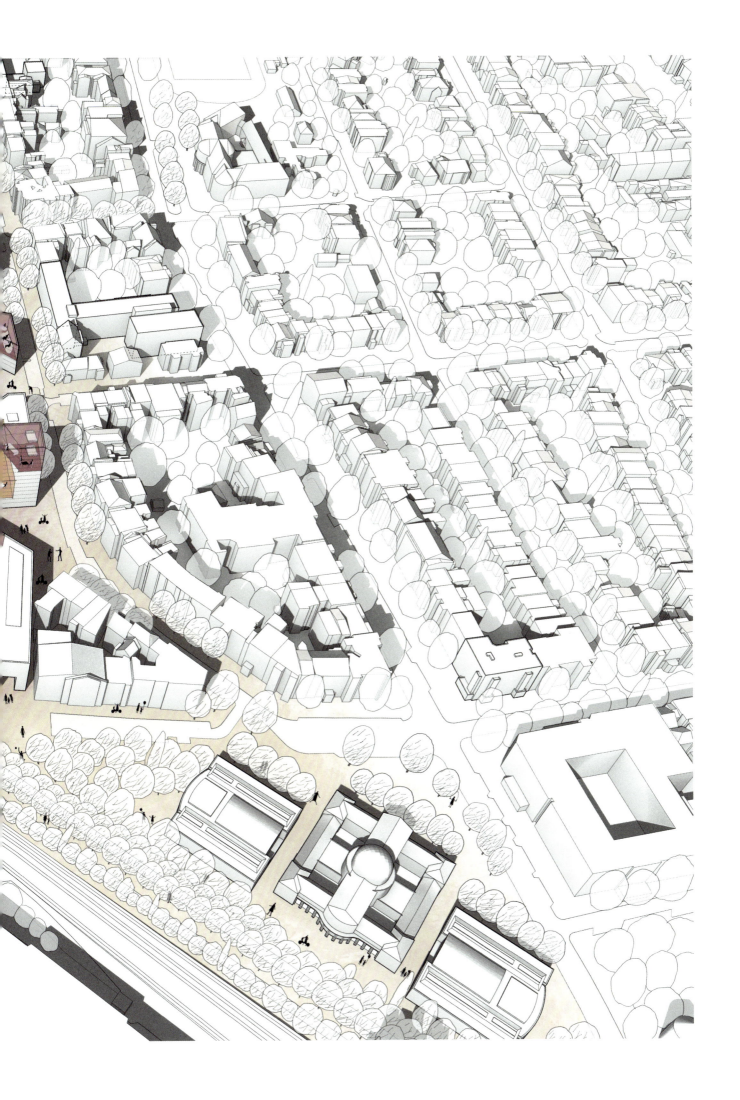

53
Von-Melle-Park: 3D model of Mosaic Scenario, views from four different directions

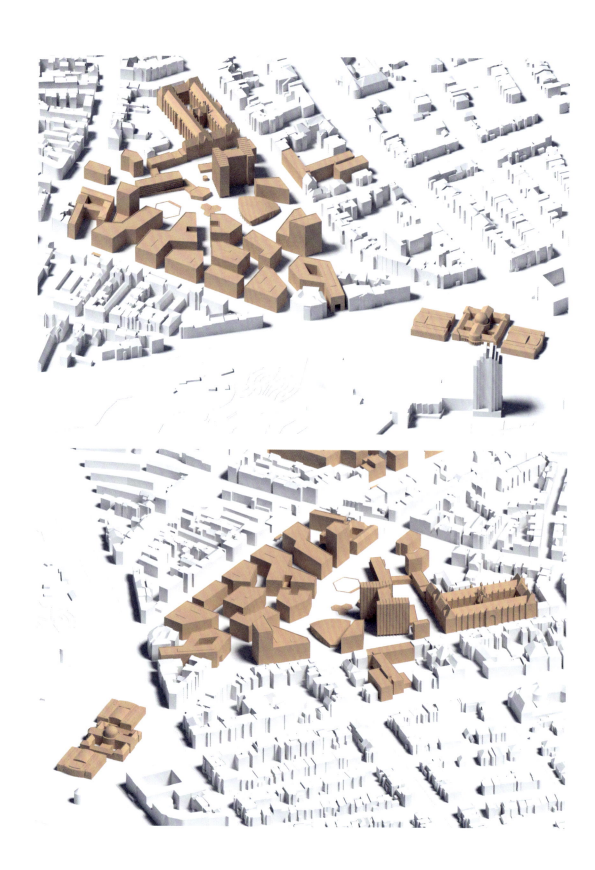

The Future | The Urban Campus: Von-Melle-Park & Bundesstraße

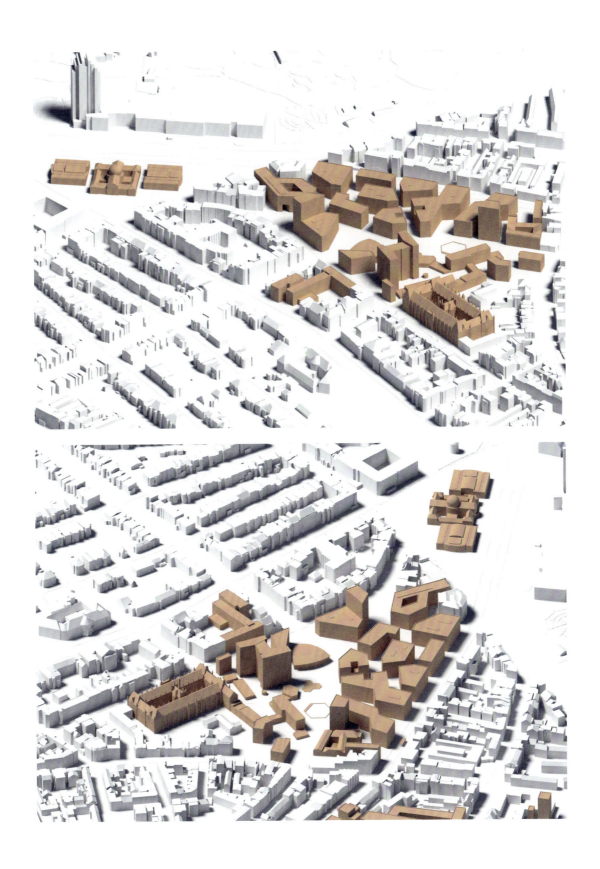

54
Bundesstraße: Visualization of Mosaic Scenario with functional areas

- Public
- Semi-public
- Internal spaces

The Future | The Urban Campus: Von-Melle-Park & Bundesstraße

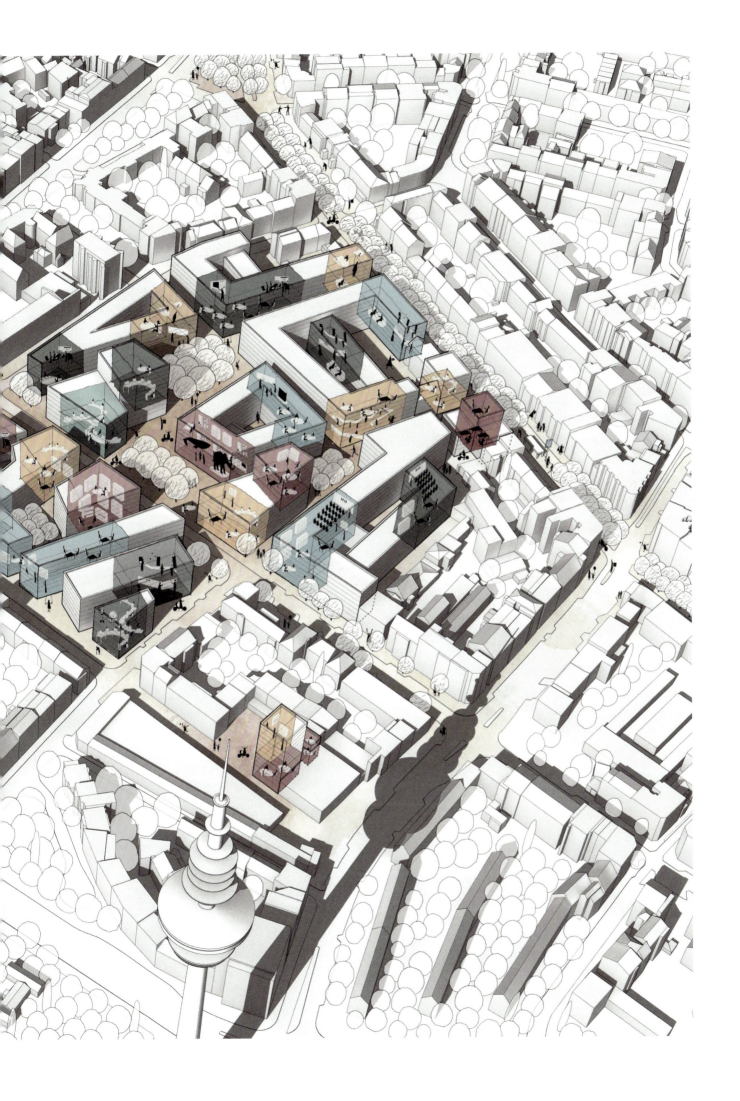

55
Bundesstraße: 3D model, Mosaic Scenario, views from four different directions

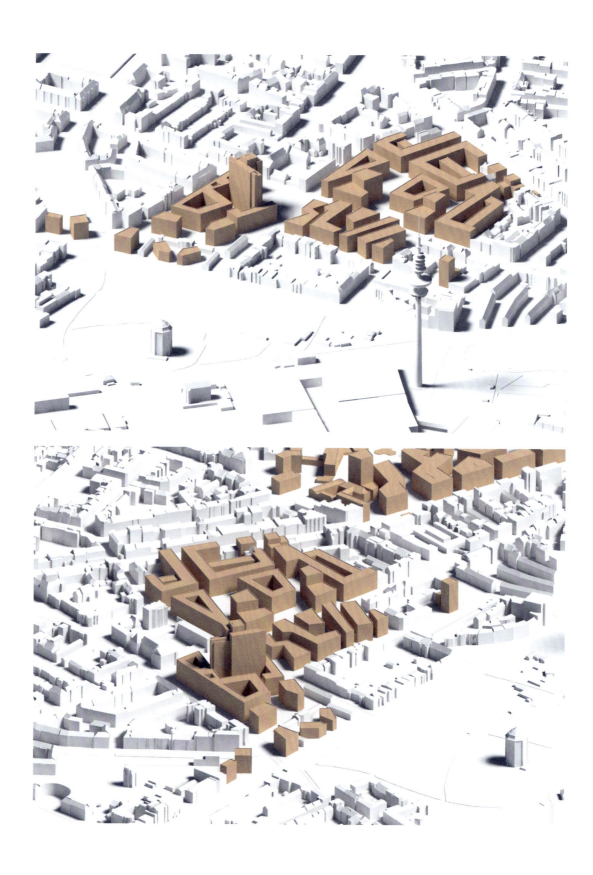

The Future | The Urban Campus: Von-Melle-Park & Bundesstraße

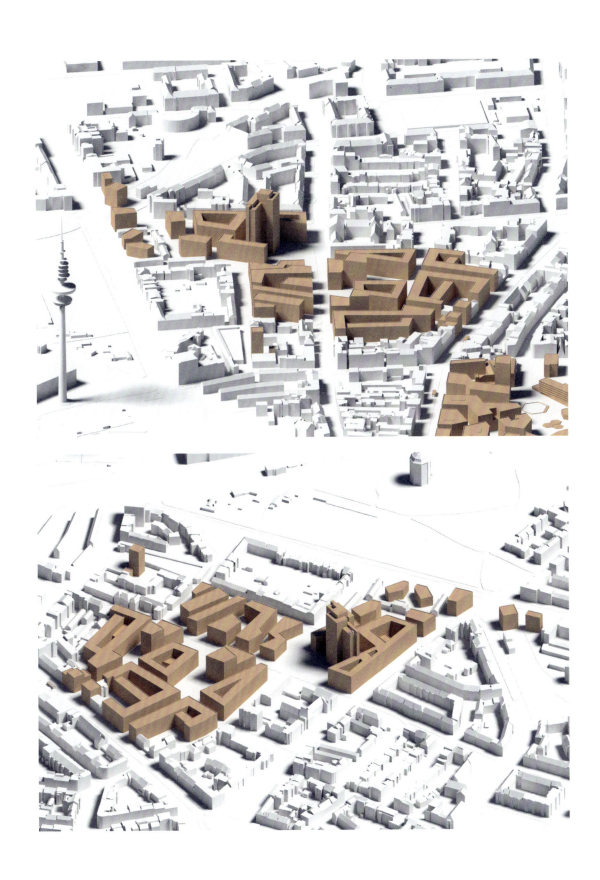

56
Urban Campus, Von-Melle-Park and Bundesstraße: Structures and outdoor spaces, Strata Scenario, M 1:10,000

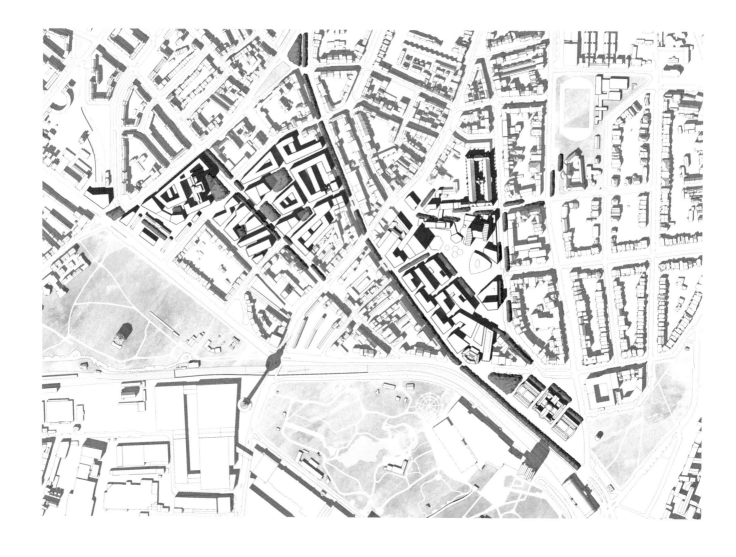

57
Urban Campus,
Von-Melle-Park and
Bundesstraße: 3D model,
Strata Scenario

58
Urban Campus, Von-Melle-Park and Bundesstraße: Axonometric view of Strata Scenario

59
Von-Melle-Park: Visualization with functional areas of Strata Scenario

- Public
- Semi-public
- Internal spaces

The Future | The Urban Campus: Von-Melle-Park & Bundesstraße

60
Von-Melle-Park: 3D model of Strata Scenario, views from four different directions

61
Bundesstraße: Visualization of Strata Scenario with functional areas

■ Public
■ Semi-public
■ Internal spaces

The Future | The Urban Campus: Von-Melle-Park & Bundesstraße

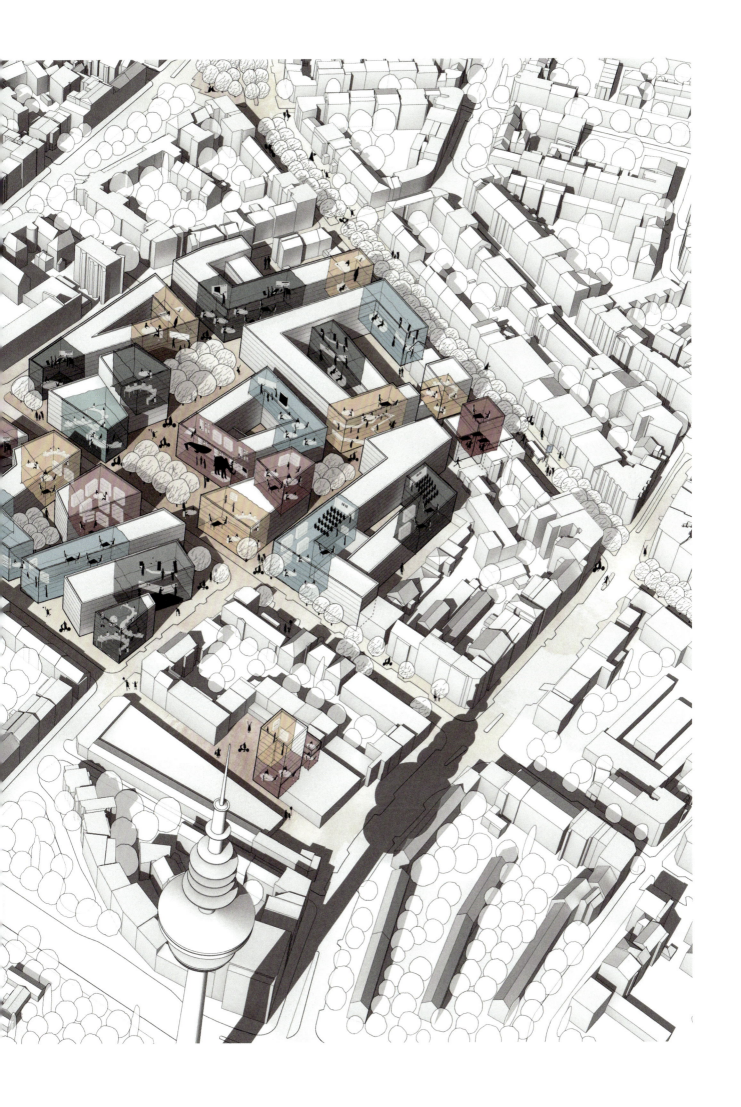

62
Bundesstraße: 3D model, Strata Scenario, views from four different directions

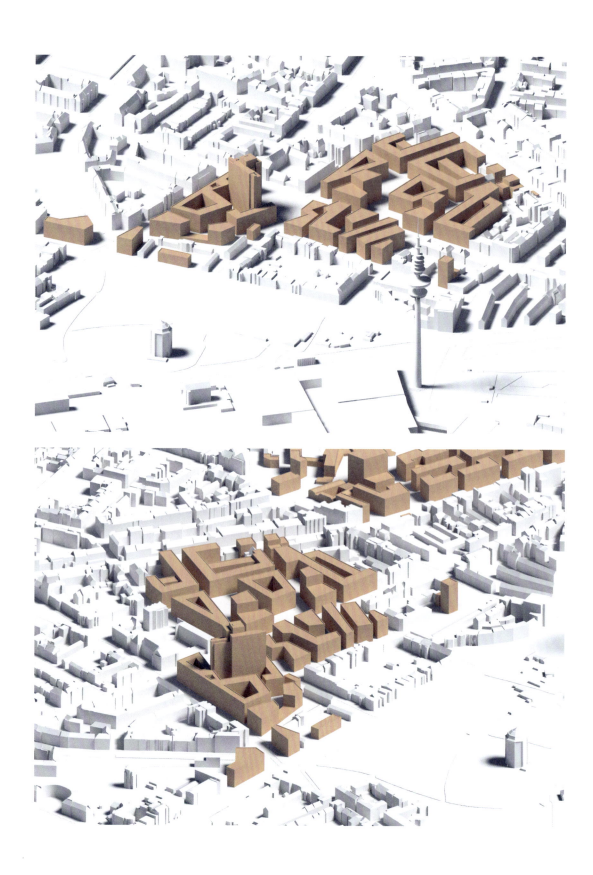

The Future | The Urban Campus: Von-Melle-Park & Bundesstraße

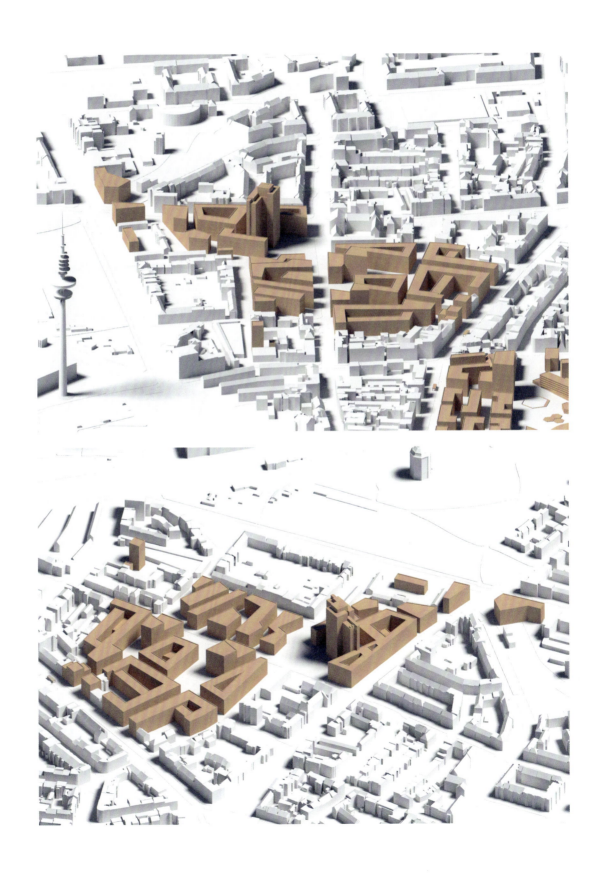

Klein Flottbek Campus

Layers – Mosaic – Strata

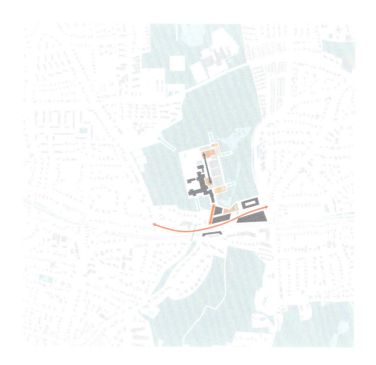

63
Universität Hamburg Urban Campus Klein Flottbek: Spatial structures and interconnections

- Core spaces
- Liminal spaces
- Internal structures
- Primary connections
- Ancillary connections

Layers

With the volume of the buildings to be constructed on Ohnhorststraße, the street is turned into the new campus boulevard for the Center for Biodiversity in Klein Flottbek. The various usages are distributed vertically within these buildings, ranging from public use on the ground floor to internal university functions on the upper levels. The largest building in this developmental scenario has atria embedded in the upper floors and replaces the current parking garage between Ohnhorststraße and the rapid transit line. The outer edges of this structure seize upon the street axes, whereas the short facade on the west side runs parallel to the path from the train station to the main entrance of the botanical gardens. One new building with a rectangular ground plan is constructed at the corner of Ohnhorststraße and Heinrich-Plett-Straße where there is currently a parking lot. To the west of that building, the main entrance to the park remains directly connected to Ohnhorststraße. Further west, and as a southern extension to the current campus development, two additional structures are erected on each side of Ohnhorststraße. The street-side facades run along the east-west axis, but the others are oriented toward the main entrance of the botanical gardens and therefore lead from the train station to the gardens. Additional new structures are also created at selected points in the direct vicinity of the current developments on this campus site and near the train station.

Mosaic

In this scenario as well, Ohnhorststraße is developed into the central boulevard of the campus. The structural masses, however, are broken up into little mosaic stones, with each building having its own specific usage on the scale ranging from external to internal. Little plaza sites emerge in a staggered pattern due to the various gaps in the mosaic structure, forming on both sides of Ohnhorststraße and toward the train station. In this scenario, there are three essential groups of mosaic stones that each encompass their own small plaza: two groups to the east, both north and south of Ohnhorststraße, and one group between the train station and the current campus development, north of Ohnhorststraße. In this scenario too, the existing campus is supplemented by new structures along the outer edges, and smaller buildings also emerge directly south of the Klein Flottbek train station.

Strata

The Strata scenario for the Klein Flottbek campus has similarities with certain parts of the Layers scenario, whereas in this case the usage is based on the strata design principle and set for the buildings on the whole. Public functions will be housed in the structures between Ohnhorststraße and the railway, where the parking garage is currently located, and in smaller new structures to the south of the station. The semi-public strata will be placed between Ohnhorststraße and the existing campus/park. In contrast to the Layers scenario, here the orientation of the facades remains consistently parallel and orthogonal to Ohnhorststraße throughout the scenario. In the area north of the train station, by slightly shifting back the new development, a forecourt is created, with its northern edge designed as a passageway to the park and the existing campus. (PF/JB)

64
Klein Flottbek: Site plan for Layers Scenario

65
Klein Flottbek: Site plan for Mosaic Scenario

66
Klein Flottbek: Site plan for Strata Scenario

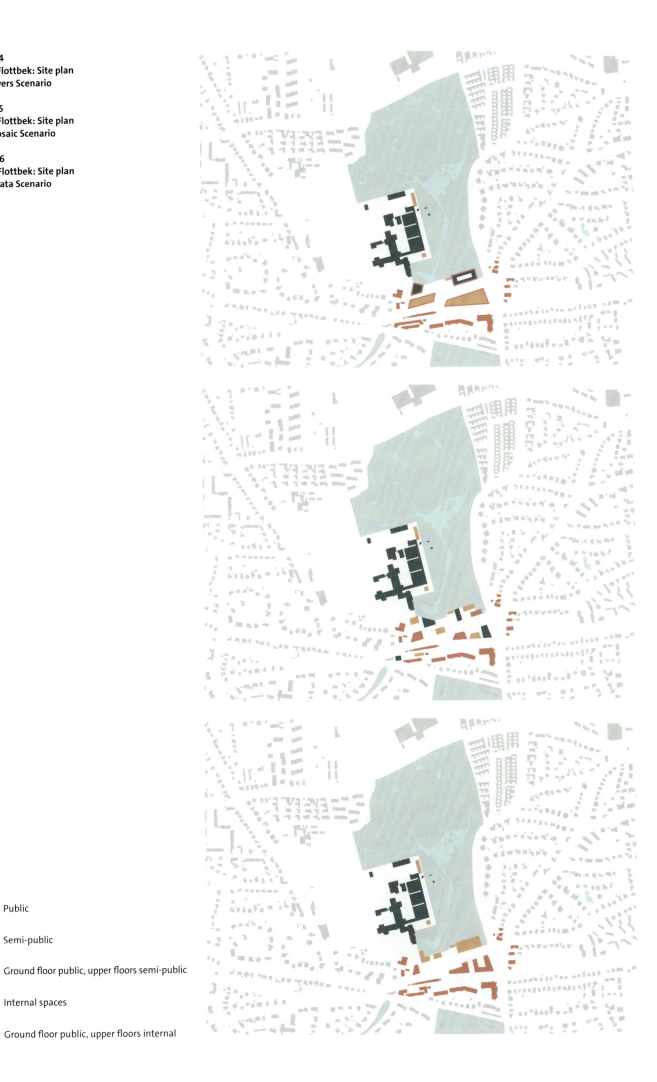

■ Public

■ Semi-public

■ Ground floor public, upper floors semi-public

■ Internal spaces

■ Ground floor public, upper floors internal

76 | 77

67
Klein Flottbek: Structures
and outdoor spaces,
Layers Scenario, M 1:10,000

68
Klein Flottbek: 3D model,
Layers Scenario

69
Klein Flottbek: Visualization of Layers Scenario with functional areas

- Public
- Semi-public
- Internal spaces

The Future | Klein Flottbek Campus

70
Klein Flottbek: 3D model, Layers Scenario, views from four different directions

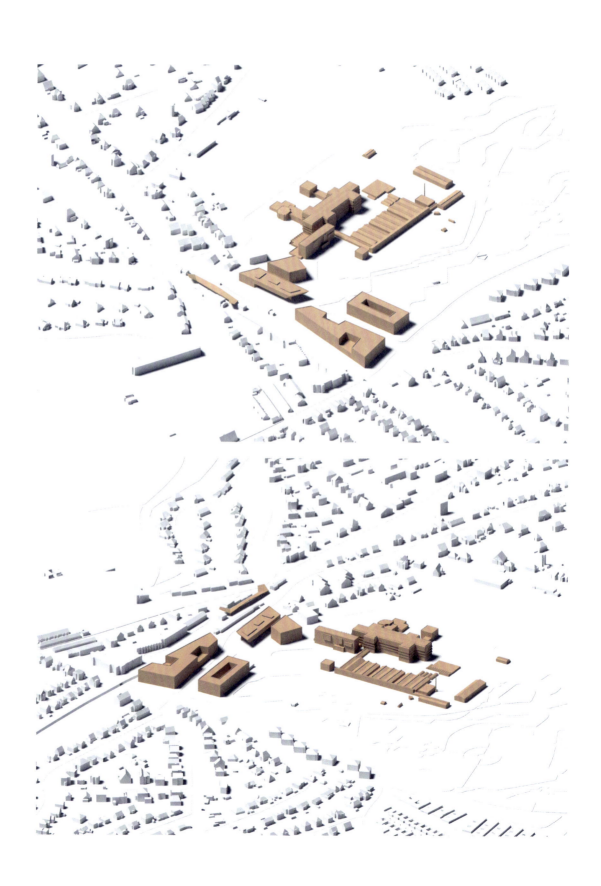

The Future | Klein Flottbek Campus

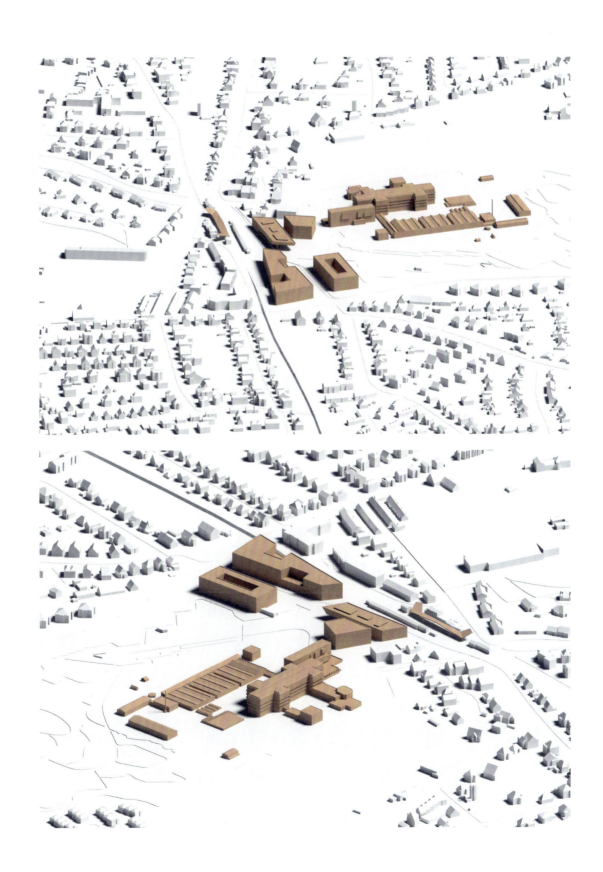

71
Klein Flottbek:
Structures and outdoor
spaces, Mosaic Scenario,
M 1:10,000

The Future | Klein Flottbek Campus

72
Klein Flottbek: 3D model,
Mosaic Scenario

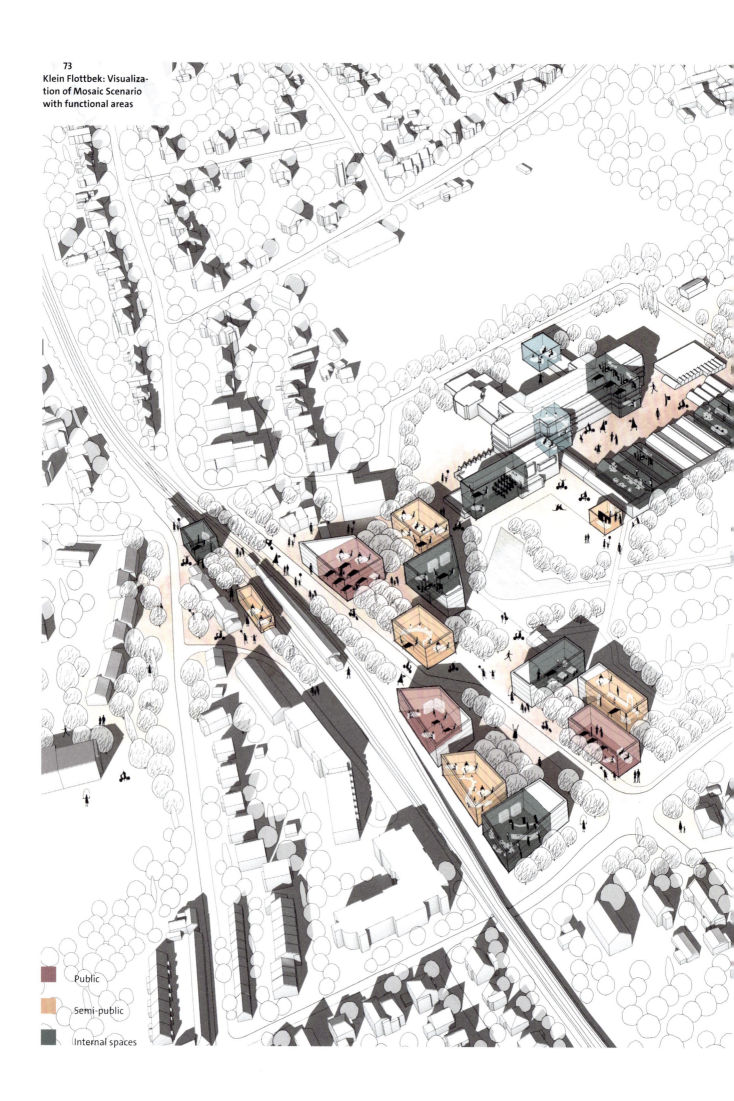

73
Klein Flottbek: Visualization of Mosaic Scenario with functional areas

- Public
- Semi-public
- Internal spaces

74
Klein Flottbek: 3D model, Mosaic Scenario, views from four different directions

The Future | Klein Flottbek Campus

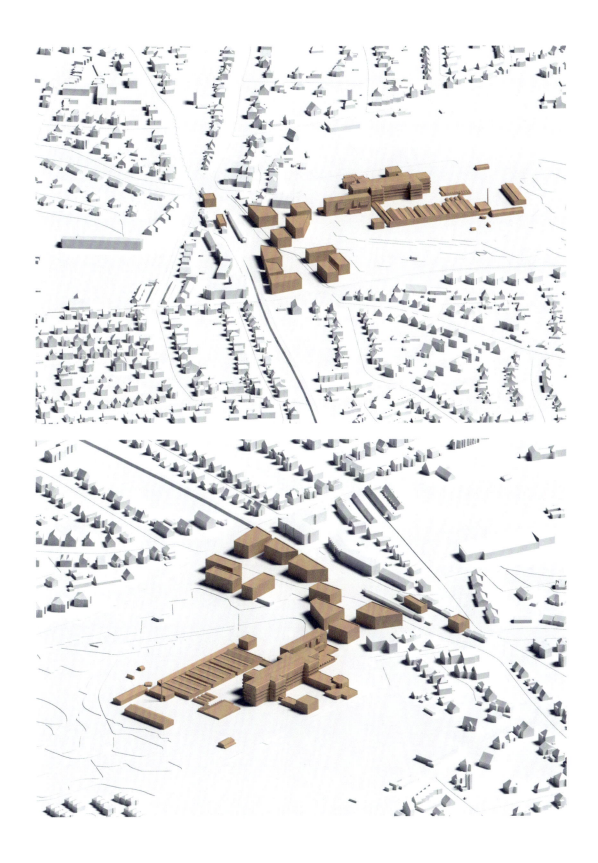

75
Klein Flottbek: Structures and outdoor spaces with functional areas, Strata Scenario, M 1:10,000

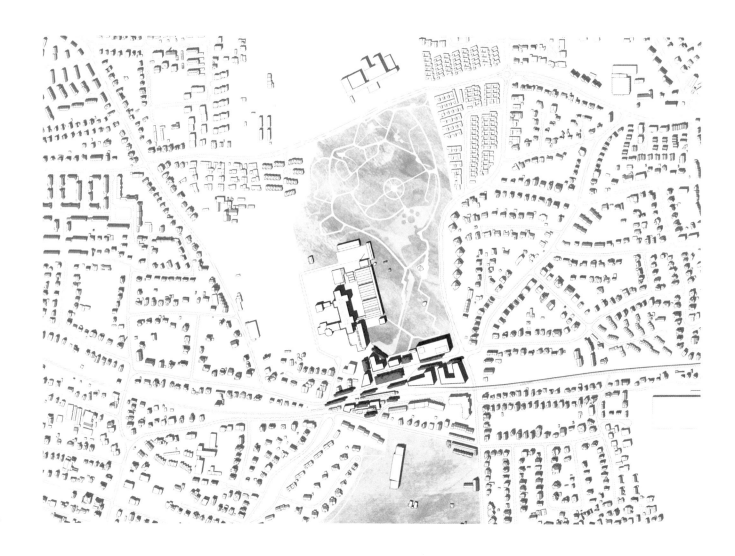

76
Klein Flottbek: 3D model,
Strata Scenario

77
Klein Flottbek: Visualization of Strata Scenario with functional areas

Public
Semi-public
Internal spaces

The Future | Klein Flottbek Campus

78
Klein Flottbek: 3D model, Strata Scenario, views from four different directions

The Future | Klein Flottbek Campus

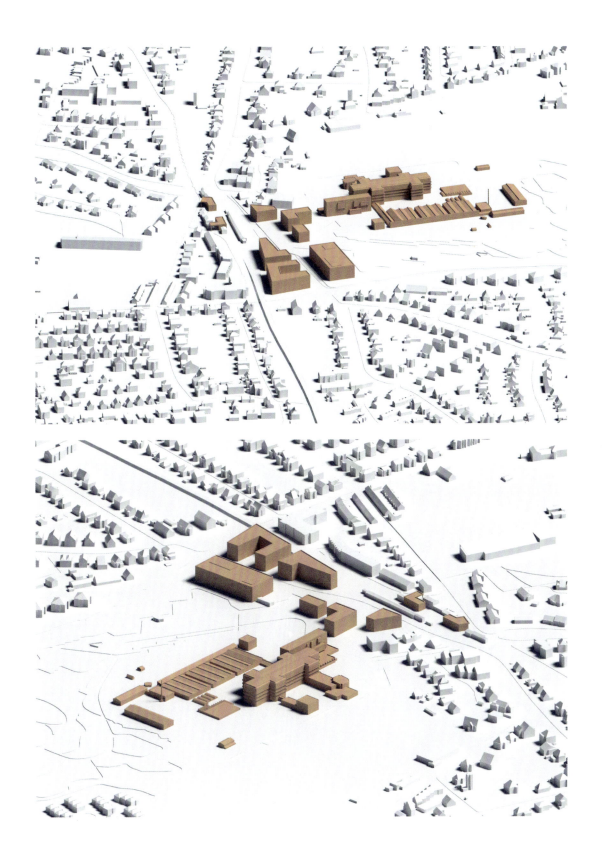

Science City Bahrenfeld

An Urban Research Campus with International Flair

79
Visualization of the concept for "Science City Bahrenfeld" with university buildings highlighted

In the future vision, the campus in the northwestern district of Hamburg, Bahrenfeld, will be transformed into a forward-thinking research site with international flair along a timeline spanning to the year 2040. The official status of the concept will be presented here, which already incorporates the principles of a "Multiple Campus" into its model.

In the fall of 2017, the German Electron Synchrotron (DESY) and Universität Hamburg, together with the Agency for Science, Research, and Equality, took the initiative to convince the First Mayor of Hamburg, Olaf Scholz, to permit the Bahrenfeld Trabrennbahn (trotting track) to be used more intensively than originally planned for the expansion of their scientific research area. Subsequently, an urban planning team developed a vision for this expansion. In January 2019, the new First Mayor, Peter Tschentscher, published the concept for "Science City Bahrenfeld,"[1] which simultaneously served as an important building block for the Universität Hamburg's strategy for excellence. It contains many essential elements of this at various levels, in terms of conceptual thought, urban design, transportation planning, and planning public space.

The point of departure for the initial development was the expansion of the campus west of the street Luruper Chaussee. Depending on planning that cannot yet entirely be foreseen, for example the exact date of the relocation of the Trabrennbahn to Horn, in the east of Hamburg, other scenarios for the initial steps in the development of Science City are also conceivable.

Although the urban design still has to be further elaborated, and architectural designs for the individual buildings are not finished yet, one thing is certain: When Science City is finally realized in its entirety, it will play a decisive role as a scientific center for a large portion of the STEM faculty, which comprises more than 5,000 students. At the same time, it will be a campus where innovative principles of a science city are implemented as a new paradigm. Science City Bahrenfeld will be a trailblazer for the social and economic development of the urban environment, and it will facilitate participation in science throughout the entire society. It will create a tightly networked city district, integrated into the surrounding urban body while also turning the city into a campus. Even at the micro-level of the individual buildings, the concept leads by example: interactive, multimedia learning areas, as spaces of encounter, will promote the development of new teaching and learning concepts.

In terms of planning the exterior space, three avenues form the central linear spaces. To the west, there is the ring of the underground particle accelerator, PETRA, circumnavigating the DESY premises, which is made visible above ground by a green ring. On the east side, there is the "Parklane" going around the Volkspark. In the middle, there is Luruper Chaussee, serving as the central public street space and as a green avenue. The most important transverse link for pedestrians and cyclists will be the "High Line," which will connect the two sections east and west of Luruper Chaussee with one another. These outdoor structures will form the backbone of the interior and exterior interconnections of the district, and furthermore, they are an essential component of the overarching network of public greenspace. Similarly, sustainable mobility is an important building block of the complete concept. Aside from creating good connections for pedestrians and cyclists within the quarter and in the surrounding districts, there are also plans to create key elements such mobility hubs, innovative shuttle systems for the internal development, as well as rapid transit connections.

In terms of urban design, the concept is composed of several individual areas. In the west, the DESY premises are supplemented by numerous new structures. In the east, within the triangle between Volkspark, Luruper Chaussee, and the highway, a new quarter emerges with residential and mixed-use buildings. In the middle, a new research campus for the Universität Hamburg will be erected on either side of Luruper Chaussee. Additionally, there are the areas adjacent to the Volkspark in the north and northwest, which are intended for businesses related to the scientific research.

The core of the university campus site is defined by its central facilities, such as a teaching and conference area at the large public plaza facing Luruper Chaussee, as well as a learning center and a cafeteria, in connection with local establishments in the district. Both parts of the campus also obtain their own public spaces, supplementary to the large plaza at Luruper Chaussee, and the facilities will be arranged around these spaces. In addition to the new university structures in the northern section of the current Trabrennbahn site, there will also be university buildings north of the central campus area, between the existing university structures and Luruper Chaussee, at the eastern entrance to the Bahrenfeld research campus, west of the commercial district on Albert-Einstein-Ring, between the research campus and Notkestraße, and at Ebertplatz as well.

Luruper Chaussee will serve as the backbone of the two sides of the campus, east and west, and as a connection to Volkspark. It will become a "science boulevard" with central scientific facilities, public campus spaces, as well as stores and restaurants for the city district. It will harbor important entryways to the campus. The scientific endeavors will directly face the street and take advantage of the visibility of this location on the main thoroughfare. Further to the southeast, Ebertplatz will become the city-side starting point for the science boulevard. It will be endowed with distinctive architecture that visualizes the themes of science and research.   (PF/JB)

---

1 Freie und Hansestadt Hamburg, Behörde für Stadtentwicklung und Wohnen: Science City Bahrenfeld – Wissenschaft lebt im Stadtteil. Hamburg, 2019

80
Visualizations of the concept for "Science City Bahrenfeld"

The Future | Science City Bahrenfeld

81
Visualizations of the concept for "Science City Bahrenfeld" from a pedestrian's perspective

The University Medical Center Hamburg-Eppendorf

The "Future Plan 2050" for the UKE

82
Site plan for the final stage of the Future Plan 2050 for the University Medical Center Hamburg-Eppendorf (UKE)

The UKE is planning its future. In order to drive forward the medical and scientific development for the benefit of the patients, the infrastructure has to be adapted to changing demands: a mammoth project with a timeline spanning to 2050.

In order for the UKE to continue providing medical treatment, conducting research, and educating students at the highest level and with international renown, ten new buildings or annexes are to be constructed on the UKE campus by the year 2050. In the first step, a new cardiovascular center will be built, along with the Martini-Clinic and second campus research center, in order to keep up with the increasing demand for more capacity, more beds, and new possibilities for research and education. Further steps include the construction of a new administrative building (the "Smart Box"), a building for storing tissue samples (the "Biobank"), an annex to the clinic for psychiatry and psychotherapy, and a new oncology center for treating cancer patients. Furthermore, by 2050, there are also plans to create a seminar and convention center, another center for campus research and education, as well as an annex for outpatients and diagnostics.

Representing the Demands of the Future, Today

"In previous years, we have already taken the step of transforming from a pavilion concept to an interdisciplinary network of university medicine under one roof. With our Future Plan 2050, we continue to build upon that. The new structures that are planned today represent the medical demands of the future," said Prof. Dr. Burkhard Göke, Medical Director and Chairman of the UKE at a press conference in August 2018.

Katharina Fegebank, Chairwoman of the Trustees of the UKE and Senator for Science, Research, and Equity, and Second Mayor of Hamburg, underscores just how significant the upcoming construction projects are for health care in the Hamburg metropolitan region: "The UKE is one of the leading hospitals in Europe, specialized in complex, serious, and rare diseases. The fact that so many people can be helped here is due to the exceptional research, excellent patient care, and the very good education provided to the next generation of healthcare professionals. The Future Plan 2050 ensures that the UKE will be able to further establish its position as a frontrunner and continue improving its range of services. All citizens of Hamburg will benefit from this."

More Than Top-Quality University Medicine

With state-of-the-art diagnostics and therapies, the UKE concentrates on researching and treating highly complex and rare diseases. Additionally, the UKE has strong partners on its premises that complement the range of healthcare services provided by the University Medical Center, for example the medical specialist clinic or the rehabilitation center, RehaCentrum Hamburg.

UKE Subsidiary is Planning and Building

The Future Plan 2050 is the central building block for the future development of the UKE. The project plans predominantly have been developed and will be implemented by KFE Klinik Facility-Management Eppendorf GmbH, a wholly owned subsidiary of the UKE. The expertise for the Future Plan 2050 is therefore not only held within the same corporation, but also located on its own campus. (SL)

83
The Future Plan 2050 for the the University Medical Center Hamburg-Eppendorf (UKE)

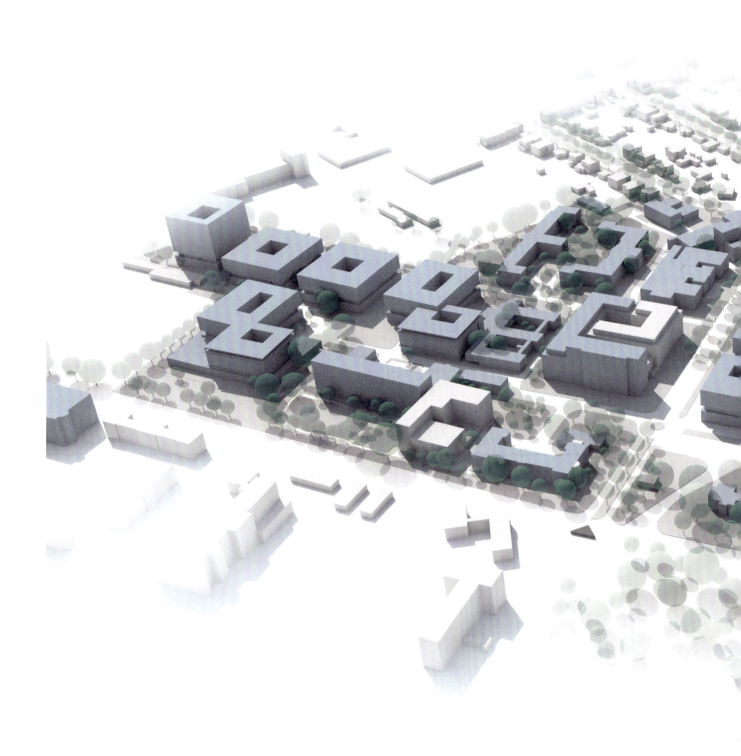

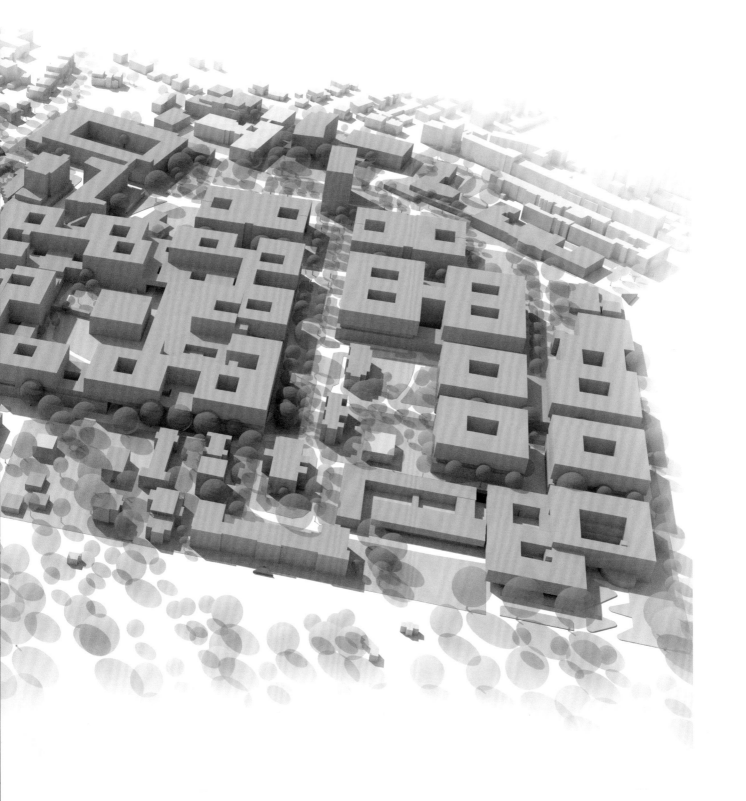

84
Interconnection and mobile accessibility of the campus sites to promote international cooperation with the Universität Hamburg

The Future

Appendix

Image Credits 110
Authors and Editors 111
Publication Information 112

Image Credits

Cover
Cover design: Kathrin Schmuck/Paul Eichholtz

Introduction
p. 6 – UHH historic main building: UHH **p. 6 – UHH main building, Agathe Lasch Lecture Hall:** UHH/Baumann **p. 6 – UHH main building, foyer, east side:** UHH/RRZ/MCC/Mentz (Photographer: Arvid Mentz) **p. 6 – Urban Campus design for Von-Melle-Park/Bundesstraße:** Chair of Urban Design, HCU Hamburg – Prof. Paolo Fusi **p. 6 – Historic aerial photograph of Von-Melle-Park:** Hamburgisches Architekturarchiv, Paul Seitz collection. Photographer: Eberhard Troeger **p. 8 – University of Amsterdam Roeterseiland Campus, cross section, view, and site plan:** AHMM Architects **p. 8 – Columbia University Manhattanville Campus, cross section and site plan:** RPBW – Renzo Piano Building Workshop Architects **p. 8 – Columbia University Manhattanville Campus, Lenfest Center for the Arts:** Frank Oudeman/Columbia University

The Future
p. 12 – 3D model: Chair of Urban Design, HCU Hamburg – Prof. Paolo Fusi **p. 14:** Public domain. (Editing: Chair of Urban Design, HCU Hamburg – Prof. Paolo Fusi) **p. 16 – Stoa of Attalos:** Public domain **p. 16 – Ed Kaplan Family Institute, floorplan:** John Ronan Architects **p. 16 – Central Saint Martins, exterior view:** John Sturrock **p. 16 – Sketch of Novartis Campus Basel:** Vittorio Magnago Lampugnani **p. 16 – Book cover Umberto Eco, Der Name der Rose:** 1982 Carl Hanser Verlag GmbH & Co. KG, München **p. 16 – Central Saint Martins, interior view:** Stanton Williams **p. 16 – TU Delft:** Paolo Fusi **p. 18 – Book cover:** © Suhrkamp Verlag AG **p. 18 – All other images on this page:** Public domain **p. 20 – St. Olav Hospital, site plan:** Nordic Office of Architecture and Ratio Architects **p. 20 – St. Olav Hospital, exterior view:** Matthias Herzog **p. 20 – Saint Gall Monastery:** Public domain **p. 20 – Teaching Center, Campus WU Vienna, site plans and exterior view:** architect BUSarchitektur (photo: BOAnet.at) **p. 22 – Exterior view, top left, and interior view:** C.F. Møller Architects/Torben Eskerod **p. 22 – Rooftop terrace:** C.F. Møller Architects/Julian Weyer **p. 22 – Floorplans:** C.F. Møller Architects **p. 24 – "Under One Roof" plans:** Kengo Kuma & Associates **p. 24 – "Under One Roof" interior view:** Michel Denancé **p. 24 – "Under One Roof" exterior view:** Alain Herzog **p. 24 – ETH courtyard:** Flickr/Benutzer Qtea, Creative Commons Attribution 2.0 Generic **p. 24 – Bottom-right image:** Unsplash/Austin Distel **p. 26 – Top-left graph:** Simon Rowberry. 2011. Vladimir Nabokov's pale fire: the lost 'father of all hypertext demos'? In: Proceedings of the 22nd ACM conference on Hypertext and hypermedia (HT, 11). ACM, New York, NY, USA, pp. 319-324. **p. 26 – Overview of strategies:** UHH **p. 26 – Atlassian Headquarters, San Francisco, California:** Studio Sarah Willmer Architecture **p. 26 – Archimedes Palimpsest:** The Walters Museum/Creative Commons Attribution 3.0 Unported **p. 28 – Futurium, exterior and interview views, center:** OBO Bettermann **p. 28 – Futurium, interior view, below:** BMBF/Hans-Joachim Rickel **p. 28 – Palmaille:** Public domain **p. 28 – MIND – Milano Innovation District:** CRA-Carlo Ratti Associati. Renderings by CRA (Gary di Silvio, Gianluca Zimbardi) and Arch 018 **p. 30 – Tietgen Residence Hall:** Lundgaard & Tranberg/Jens Lindhe **p. 30 – Rolex Learning Center, floorplan:** SANAA **p. 30 – Rolex Learning Center, exterior view:** Alain Herzog/EPFL **p. 30 – Book cover:** Mario Milizia, Sottsass Associati **p. 32 – Ed Kaplan Family Institute, exterior view:** Steve Hall © Hall + Merrick+ McCaugherty **p. 32 – Ed Kaplan Family Institute, floorplan:** John Ronan Architects **p. 34 – Ed Kaplan Family Institute, plans:** John Ronan Architects **p. 34 – Ed Kaplan Family Institute, interior views:** Steve Hall © Hall+ Merrick+ McCaugherty **p. 34 – Kernareal USZ, plans:** Christ & Gantenbein **p. 34 – S. R. Crown Hall:** Illinois Institute of Technology **p. 34 – The Forum, cross section:** Renzo Piano Building Workshop **p. 34 – Manhattanville Campus, view from south:** Frank Oudeman/Columbia University **pp. 38-95 – All images:** Chair of Urban Design, HCU Hamburg – Prof. Paolo Fusi **p. 96:** City of Hamburg – Ministry of Urban Development and Housing/Spengler Wiescholek Architekten Stadtplaner, Urban Catalyst GmbH, WES GmbH Landschaftsarchitekten (edited) **pp. 98/99:** City of Hamburg – Ministry of Urban Development and Housing/Spengler Wiescholek Architekten Stadtplaner, Urban Catalyst GmbH, WES GmbH Landschaftsarchitekten **p. 100/101 – Visualizations:** moka-studio **p. 102 – Monochrome plan:** Johannes Bouchain (Map data: City of Hamburg, State Ministry for Geo-Information and Surveying, License: Germany – Attribution – Version 2.0/UKE) **pp. 104/105:** UKE **pp. 106/107 – Graphic design:** Kathrin Schmuck/Paul Eichholtz. (Small graphics in the circles: Chair of Urban Design, HCU Hamburg – Prof. Paolo Fusi; City of Hamburg – Ministry of Urban Development and Housing/Spengler Wiescholek Architekten Stadtplaner, Urban Catalyst GmbH, WES GmbH Landschaftsarchitekten; UKE)

Unless otherwise noted, all plans, visualizations, and models are oriented to the north.

We thank all copyright holders for the permission to reproduce their images in this publication. Despite intensive efforts, errors or omissions cannot be entirely ruled out. In order to clarify any potential copyright claims, we request that you contact the author.

Authors and Editors

Author

Professor Paolo Fusi
Chair of Urban Design
HafenCity Universität Hamburg

Guest Contributor

Saskia Lemm
Spokeswoman
UKE Medical Center
Hamburg-Eppendorf

Editors

Johannes Bouchain
Urban Planner
Stadtkreation

Dr. Martin Hecht
Chancellor
Universität Hamburg

Professor Paolo Fusi
Chair of Urban Design
HafenCity Universität Hamburg

Eva Liesberg
Architect
Universität Hamburg
Department 8 – Property Management
Section 86 – Campus Development

Kathrin Schmuck
Bucharchitektur \ Kathrin Schmuck

Marita Vietmeyer
Architect
Universität Hamburg
Department 8 – Property Management
Section 86 – Campus Development

Publication Information

Publisher
Universität Hamburg
HafenCity Universität Hamburg

Author
Prof. Paolo Fusi

Guest Contributor
Saskia Lemm

Editors
Johannes Bouchain (Urban Planner)
Dr. Martin Hecht
Prof. Paolo Fusi
Eva Liesberg (Architect)
Kathrin Schmuck
Marita Vietmeyer (Architect)

Concept and Design
Bucharchitektur \ Kathrin Schmuck

Assistance
Stefanie Ammann Fusi, Nicolai Bouchain, Susanne Buckler, Paolo Burattini, Celia Dahmen, Paul Eichholtz, Hendrik Koch, Jasmin Liska, Mohamad Sankari, Andrea Tomasino

Lithography
Bild1Druck, Berlin

Translation
Theodore Kuttner

Printing and Binding
optimal media GmbH, Röbel/Müritz

Paper
Munken Lynx 130 g/qm

Binding
Peyvida puro 350 g/qm

© 2024 Universität Hamburg & HafenCity Universität Hamburg
The rights to the texts belong to the respective authors. The image rights belong to their respective owners. All rights reserved.

Bibliographic information published by the Deutsche Nationalbibliothek. The Deutsche Nationalbibliothek lists this publication in the Deutsche Nationalbibliographie; detailed bibliographic data are available on the Internet at www.dnb.d-nb.de

This publication is based on the German-language book: Multiple Campus. Szenarien für die Universität der Zukunft, published by JOVIS Verlag, Berlin, 2019.
www.jovis.de

ISBN 978-3-947972-71-5
eISBN 978-3-947972-72-2

This publication was made possible by the support of the HafenCity Universität Hamburg in the context of the cooperative project for campus development.